Polarities of Power

Raven Kaldera

Polarities of Power

Energy Work for Power Dynamic Relationships

Raven Kaldera

Alfred Press
Hubbardston, Massachusetts

Alfred Press
12 Simond Hill Road
Hubbardston, MA 01452

Polarities of Power: Energy Work for Power Dynamic Relationships
© 2018 Raven Kaldera
ISBN 978-0-9905441-3-5

Printed in cooperation with
Lulu Enterprises, Inc.
860 Aviation Parkway, Suite 300
Morrisville, NC 27560

Dedicated to my darling slaveboy Joshua
and to Brandon, dog and chela
who helped me to learn so much about this path.

Contents

Introduction: Dominance, Submission, and Energy

The genesis of this book started many years ago, when my slaveboy Joshua and I were first together. I'm a shaman who does a lot of energy work professionally, and of course I would often incorporate it into my sex life. However, it wasn't until I took up with Joshua that I found a partner who was equally interested, and who wasn't frightened when I would play with our energy bodies during sex in order to enhance the experience. We both became interested in Tantric sexual techniques, and we looked into some of the traditional techniques as a way to find even more ways to do this with each other.

However, we are both transgendered — not to mention being a same-sex couple — and nearly all the Tantric energy-sex training was extremely heterocentric. A few books and groups focused on gay Tantra, but mostly it seemed to suggest that one person had to play the "woman's part" and another had to play the "man's part". The well-meaning Tantrikas that we spoke to had no idea what to do with us. They encouraged us to experiment and figure it out ourselves, and we did. We formed a group of transgendered explorers, and we met monthly to discuss possible energy-sex experiments, go home and try them with our various partners, and report back.

During our experiments, Joshua and I played around with our sexual gender roles, and the genders of our energy body, trying every combination we could think of — for research purposes, of course! We noticed one thing, however. Removing "gender" — or, at least the traditional roles applied to dual-gendered sex — from the equation meant that our "energy sex" followed a different path. It brought other opposing traits more strongly into play, and the energy followed those routes — most obviously that of our D/s polarity. (Although occasionally it eddied about, foregrounding our age difference.) We learned something important from that work: first, that energy sex really does work better when there is an opposite polarity between two people ... and second, that polarity absolutely does not have to be gender.

In fact, even for heterosexual people who have a power dynamic relationship, the flow of dominance and submission between them is just as powerful a polarity as heterosexual gender. It was an "Aha!" moment for us: any opposing qualities between two people that can be eroticized will work to create that energy. It could be extrovert/introvert, soft-bodied/hard-bodied, quiet and mysterious opposed to loud and brash. It didn't seem to matter what they were, so long as both people in question got a sexual thrill out of them. For us, with our master/slave relationship as the most important defining factor, our energy sex quickly arranged itself along those lines. As a same-sex trans couple, we were easily able to pick apart "dominant" and "submissive" from "male" and "female", where they'd been socially stuck together for far too long. We began to observe what ways of moving energy — and, more specifically, doing energy work on each other — flowed better between us when we arranged ourselves in identifiably dominant or submissive modes or positions. These usually also helped strengthen our dynamic on an emotional level ... and they were damn hot, too.

I should take a short detour and explain what I meant by "Tantra", and why we are not using that term to refer to the contents of this book. In a general sense, Tantra refers to a diverse and mutually contradictory assortment of Indian philosophies and practices which hold that the material world is a concrete manifestation of the divine. While most forms of Tantra are not specifically focused on sexuality, they generally embrace the idea that the entirety of our human experience has the potential to be a venue to experience the sacred. There is often an emphasis on embracing the sacredness of things normally considered "spiritually impure" and rejecting limiting social conventions. A subset of these specifically incorporate sexual techniques in their spiritual practice, but in a traditional context, sexuality is not the primary focus.

What we are talking about in this book is specifically the energetic and spiritual component of a practice that uses the emotional flows of dominance and submission as pathways. While this could arguably be called a Tantric sort of practice, we have too much respect for the actual traditional practice of Tantra to use that term for what we're describing here. We are also rather chagrined to see how so little of what is claimed to be "Tantra" actually has any resemblance at all to the traditional practice, and we don't want to add to that pile of inaccuracy.

We're also not going to be focusing entirely on the practices of SM and kinky sex. In fact, most of the exercises in this book will not be sexual, although they may be psychologically erotic for some people. These days, some SM players are figuring out that exchanging energy in various ways during a scene can be a thrilling and bonding activity; they mostly refer to this as "energy play". However, we also want to explode the fallacy that all power dynamic relationships come out of a BDSM practice and necessarily include SM or other activities that are traditionally considered to be kinky sex. This isn't a book about sexual techniques; it's a book about ways for people in power dynamic relationships to do energy work, using their power polarity as a way to deepen the connection and make the work more effective. Everything in here can be utilized by people who never do SM, bondage, or anything more than vanilla-appearing sex. Some activities, of course, will revolve around a specific fetish, but they can be adapted to fit your own lives.

At this point, especially if your familiarity with any kind of energy work is either pseudo-Tantra or SM, you may be asking why anyone would bother to do this sort of thing if not for sexual reasons. There are actually many reasons why people do energy work on each other, but this book focuses on the positive results that it has on a Master/slave relationship, if it is pressed into service. Working with each others' energy modifies behavior over time, for one thing. Its effects can reverberate through the psyche in ways that can strongly bond two people, and bind them into a particular way of being with each other.

That brings us to one final warning. This is heavy stuff. It forges psychic bonds between people, and we don't mean that metaphorically. This is not something to be done casually, or when a relationship is new. Until time has proven that the commitment is going to work out, be careful what kind of psychic chains you build between you. They won't necessarily keep each other from leaving, but it will make a breakup far more painful and drawn-out than it would be otherwise, and require a much longer recovery time. You don't want to be one of the people who ends up in the office of someone like Raven, asking them to energetically remove the bond with their ex so that they can get on with their life. Go into this work understanding that it will create an intimacy that is too deep to walk away from easily ... and choose your partners very, very carefully.

Experiencing energy can be the a slightly tangible "hum", but mostly it is a "sensing", a "being aware of" something that cannot be seen, tasted, heard, touched or smelled, yet you know it is there. A friend of years ago called it her "spidey sense", and I agree. It's as if there's another sense along with those other five. In my experience, we all have this ability. Some are more aware of it and/or have developed it more than others have, but anyone can be taught if they wish. Energy never dies, nor is it created, but it moves around and can be moved around, inside and outside the body. It can be built up or lessened, can be held and released, can be sent and received, and can be exchanged and blended.

I have become aware of different types of energy over the years. My first experience of my own energy and of the energy outside me was when I was about five. My experience — not a metaphor but my actual experience — is that first there's my own energy; that almost imperceptible hum that exists in my body that I can move around, build and lessen, send to another. Then there's the energy of another, and then the energy of a place. I can also receive those energies, or block them. Also, there's the energy from above, which I call cosmic energy, and the energy of this planet which I call earth energy. Mostly cosmic energy is light, bright, and sparkly, and earth is deep, dark, and, well, earthy.

When I couldn't go to sleep at night around age eight, I began experimenting, "playing" with that hum, and building it, lessening it, moving it around in my body. I found that if I breathed fast in short breaths I could increase it. I also found that if I was breathing deeply and slowly the energy was easier to move than if I was breathing shallowly. Then I was a teenager, and I could stay up later so I fell asleep more quickly, and my "practice" tapered off and then ended. The knowledge, however, stayed with me.

In 1967, when I was 17 the concept of vibrations or "vibes" ("...that place is full of bad vibes," "...he has good vibes," "...don't bad vibe me, man!") was coming into the hippie counter-culture. Drugs like LSD, mescaline, peyote, etc. reconnected me with and enhanced my energetic abilities. At first I thought it was just a combination of my imagination and the drugs during a trip, but afterwards my abilities still had been somehow ... refined. For one thing, not only did I sense the hum, but I was aware of energy without the hum. Drugs only went so far, however. Around that time I discovered that I could push my "vibes" (hum, energy, etc.) out of me, and wrap a cocoon of it around someone when they were upset, and they would calm down. I also used it to establish rapport with people, although I wouldn't have phrased it like that; back then I'd have said I was "tuning into their vibes". I also used it for sex — blocking people who were interested in me when I wasn't into them, touching people I was interested in, and connecting and merging when being sexual or sensual.

As I had no formal training, it didn't occur to me then to get verbal or even psychic consent, or to tell people what I was doing. In my mind, I was doing no harm to another; I didn't throw bolts of nasty stuff, I didn't connect to them in order to do harm. But, for example, I didn't know to separate out the energies when we were done, or leave people alone if they didn't want my energetic "help", no matter what dire condition they might be in. However, in 1980 I joined the Society of Janus in San Francisco. People were talking about "the energy" of a scene, a person, or a style of play, and it all began to click inside me. I began researching: erotic energy, libido, ch'i, etc. There was no internet then, so it was all books and conversation. One of the first things I learned was that I am a natural transmitter, and what I needed to learn more about was how to listen. I also learned about consent. In the mid-1980s, I became aware of Wicca, Tantra, and energy work in general. I read a lot more, and in 1997 I received my Reiki II attunements. Today I still "tune in" with people, but now it is all done with prior consent.

In my D/s relationships, I specifically do the following with my subjects: If they are upset or challenged and need to be contained, I still wrap them in energy. I might check their first chakra and their grounding cord, and if I sense they need to be grounded, I verbally encourage them to be aware of its position and let it drop down into the earth. If I sense they aren't able to do that, I might throw a floor of stabilizing energy underneath them. I might contact their chakras with mine and see how stable, strong, weak, resistant, and willing that connection is. I might then contact their chakras with mine, establish an energetic bridge or cord, and clean and balance their chakras.

I teach all my partners, even those I've played with only once at a party, a couple of breathing, visualization, and energetic techniques to allow them to have an experience of bringing down energetic blocks. I show them what it's like to have outside energy rushing up through their body and out their head, causing their body to undulate like a dolphin on my table. This is demonstrably repeatable even with total strangers. I speak with my subjects (and anyone and everyone else) about energy, so that we can all consciously, consensually and actively participate in the flow.

–Sybil Holliday

Definitional Hell

As in, we descend into it. These are the words that we'll be using in this book. You may not use these definitions, but for the sake of consistency and clear communication, this is how we use them.

Power Dynamic: A relationship between two or more consenting adults where an imbalance of authority has been previously openly negotiated over at least some outside-the-bedroom, real-life areas of someone's life.

Dominant/submissive (or D/s): A power dynamic relationship where the "dominant" party has negotiated authority over limited areas of the "submissive" partner's outside-the-bedroom real life.

Master/slave: A power dynamic relationship where the "master" (which we use to refer to either gender) has negotiated authority over the majority of the areas of the "slave" partner's life.

Owner/property: A power dynamic relationship where the "owner" has negotiated complete and effective control over all parts of the "property" partner's life.

(Where are the boundaries between these different sorts of relationships? We aren't going to hash that out here. We aren't the power exchange police; you decide for yourself what kind of relationship you have, including throwing these definitions out the window and using your own, or deciding not to label your power dynamic at all. You know yourselves best; you figure it out. Also, please note that we will be skipping back and forth between these terms when we're describing specific activities, as in "The master will start breathing..." and it's up to you and your own judgment to pick out the Side In Charge and the Side That Takes Orders and mentally relabel them in order to be comfortable for yourselves.)

Top/bottom: In sex or a BDSM scene, the individual acting on the other, and the individual being acted on. May or may not be related to any power dynamic, in the scene or the relationship.

Scene: This has two separate meanings. The most popular one indicates one discrete episode of (usually kinky, often theatrical) sex, as in "We had a scene last night and it was lots of fun." Another more obscure meaning is a reference to one's local BDSM community, as in "We've been in the scene for four years now."

Energy: The psychic "life force" that flows through the world, including in many things we would think of as inanimate objects. It is referred to as *mana, prana, chi, ki, orgone, huna, ond,* and by many other names in other languages and cultures. (Modern English is an anomaly for not having a specialized word for it.) Energy becomes "flavored" by the nature of what it is currently flowing through — the energy in your aura and body is you-flavored, with additional "shading" of your current mood and physical state. The energy of the local lake is water-flavored, with additional "shading" of the condition of that lake's ecosystem, and its general personality, and so forth. Energy can be moved around, in your body and outside of it, with education and practice.

Energy body: The roughly-you-shaped field of energy taking up the space inside your physical body, as opposed to your "aura" which is the field surrounding your body and taking up your personal space. (Think of it this way: "Energy body" is to "aura" as "planet" is to "atmosphere".) Everyone's energy body is different; most strongly resemble the physical body, but many don't. Most are fairly well-defined, but some are more vague and shapeless. Most stay relatively stable in form, but some shift around frequently, with or without the person's knowledge and control. There is no "right way" to have an energy body; we are all individuals with different factors affecting our lives. For a good summary of the nature of energy bodies, Joshua Tenpenny's essay on the subject (originally from the book *Hermaphrodeities*) has been reprinted in the appendix section.

On Binaries and Polarities

In the somewhat radical relationship circles in which I often travel, the concept of binary polarities — identifying two traits that are opposite in any two given people, things, or situations — is somewhat suspect. Radicals point to the way that society tries to separate people into Good People and Bad People, depending on a host of traits that aren't necessarily positive or negative in and of themselves, except for the social opprobrium attached to them — homosexual/heterosexual, female/male, fat/thin, black/white, poor/rich, transgendered/monogendered, disabled/able-bodied, etc. Sometimes they blame the concept of binaries themselves, and wish that we could get rid of all binaries. More conservative folks often rebel against that idea, but they rarely seem to have an articulate concept of why binaries are important, except that "...I kinda like them," or "...they just *are*." This is sometimes seen by radicals as an attempt to defend the social benefits that any one of them might get from being on the "good" side of the binary, when in actuality there may be another reason entirely which is being missed. Especially when it comes to sex, and sexual attraction.

As I mentioned in the introduction, Joshua and I stumbled upon our practice of power-dynamic energy polarity through an attempt to get beyond the polarity of gender in traditional practices of sex magic. What we — and our compatriots in the work — discovered, as I described, was that binaries are important to sex, because they create immediate energy to work with, and that energy is easier to direct and pass back and forth. (Indeed, "back" and "forth" is a binary right there.) Focusing on "same" can also create energy, but it is a more static energy that is harder to move around — it tends to revert to stasis if you don't keep stirring it up, and the more you stir it around (so to speak), the more you risk introducing its opposite and creating a polarity anyway.

I have a strong background in astrology, so my view of how the Universe works is definitely influenced by the astrological worldview. In astrology, it is accepted that "same" is sometimes harmonious and sometimes dissonant, and that "different" can also fall into either category. For example, there are four "elements" (Air, Fire, Water, Earth, which are shorthand for mind-centered, action-centered, emotion-centered, or physicality-centered) and three "modalities" (Cardinal, Fixed, and Mutable, which indicate wanting to lead, wanting to stay in one place, or wanting to move about freely). Any two planets in someone's astrological chart will have their own elements and modalities. It is understood that planets in the same element (or elements which are "friendly" to each other, e.g. Air/Fire or Water/Earth) will be harmonious, while clashing elements will have trouble. On the other hand, planets in the same modality will clash, while those in different modalities will be more harmonious together. In anyone's astrological chart, the geometric angles between planets that fall into the first category will be the parts of them that naturally work well together, while those that fall into the second category will be their internal arguments between clashing urges.

As an example, imagine that two people share the same trait: stubbornness. While it is possible, with a great effort of will, to bring their mutual stubbornness to bear together positively on a single goal, that will take a lot of effort and mindfulness. On a day-to-day basis, it's likely that their stubbornness will result in constant clashes. It's been said many times: sometimes people don't get along because of the ways in which they are different, and sometimes people don't get along because of the ways in which they are the same.

In my mind, these days, I divide binaries into two rough groups. (How's that for binary-ing one's binaries?) On one side, I put what I call the "judgment binaries" — good/bad, better/worse, valuable/valueless, useful/useless, desirable/undesirable, etc. On the other side I put *every other binary in existence.* As part of my personal spiritual discipline of relationship (and of looking at the world), I strive to allow myself to experience the other binaries *without putting one of the judgment binaries on top of it.* I have come to believe that it's not the binaries that are the problem; it is that we are taught as children to stick a judgment binary on top of every other binary we come across. Sometimes we have to fumble around and prevaricate in order to figure out which side gets which judgment, but once it's stuck, it's hard for us to unstick it. We cling to that concept even when we find ourselves in circumstances where it's obvious that it's not true, or that we need to embrace the side we previously considered to be negative.

As I look at the world and the way in which we've used binaries as a stick to beat people with, it becomes ever more clear to me that the problem isn't binaries themselves; it's that we are taught to use them in unskillful ways. Sticking a value judgment on top of every binary you run across is unskillful. It's a crutch to keep from actually experiencing the binary in its pure essence, irrelevant to which side we have more affinity for or personal investment in. To attempt to throw binaries out the window is like saying no one should get married because half end up divorced ... or, on a more specific level, that no one should be polyamorous because most people fail on the first try, having no available models to tell them how to avoid common mistakes. Instead, there is a lot more honor in making an effort to teach people skills, so that they don't fail — and learning to experience polarities without judging one as better than the other is a necessary skill to have if you are playing with deliberate use of sexual energy. It's a great discipline for the rest of life as well, but it's especially crucial for this work. Why? Because you cannot cleanly work with the energy of a sexual polarity if you feel less than wholly positive about both your side and your partner's side.

So how does one go about creating a discipline of mindfulness and skill around polarities? I'll tell you up front that it takes a while. I've been trying it for years and I still slip up, but it's worth doing the long-term work to deprogram yourself. I recommend trying the exercises below as part of developing your spiritual discipline in this area. (Don't think it sounds particularly spiritual? Try these for a year and see what it does to your sense of spirituality. I dare you. Don't think you're a particularly spiritual person? Try these for a year and then see what's happened to your sense of yourself as having or not having a spiritual practice. In fact, try making "spiritual/mundane" one of your first binaries. I double dare you.)

Pick one pair of traits that are opposite polarities — in people, or things, or situations. Just one to begin with; don't go overboard. For example, you could decide that today is "hard/soft" — what ways can you see that polarity playing out in life around you today, or in your internal process? Sit with each pairing and visualize some version of it where neither side is "good" or "bad", but where both sides have their own equal value, or are beyond value — day and night, for example, can be experienced as just part of nature, without any need to lay any sort of value on them. If you find yourself attempting to lay a judgment, stomp on that and reorient your thoughts once again to experiencing the polarity without laying that judgment. Tomorrow, pick another new binary and work on it.

After you've worked through some of the more obvious binaries, try working on some that are opposite qualities between yourself and your partner, if you have one. Try one that is positive, that "dances" together well. The next day, try one that causes trouble between you. The day after that, try one that is eroticizable. (These exercises are enlightening to do with your partner, sharing the ideas that come up through your separate visualizations.)

Once you've gone through at least fifty binaries, it's time to start dealing with the space between them. Pick the first binary you did, and visualize the point in between, that is neither fully one nor the other, but partakes of both. Spend the next several days finding and experiencing the liminal space in the center of those binaries.

Now spend time experiencing the binary of liminal/polarized without judgment. Note any difficulties you have with this exercise; it's all right to come back to it a few times. After this, go back and pull up binaries where you had difficulty seeing the both/and space as problematic, and let yourself sit with it in a more nonjudgmental space, applying what you learned in struggling with the lesson of liminal/polarized.

Now that you've gone through all that, you can more cleanly come to the polarities that you and your partner use as erotic attraction. Discuss these with your partner; talk about how you manifest those during sex. Do they come out through actions or behavior, or is it more of a general awareness that your partner has that trait?

These exercises require nothing but your own mind, and can be done on the bus, or while stuck in traffic, or sitting in the doctor's office surrounded by nothing but bad magazines. Ideally, you should try it on a daily basis. Once you've begun, you'll notice the Universe presenting you with binaries to consider, because the Powers That Be notice these things, and want to help you in your journey of personal evolution.

The Ethics of Energy Work

Before we go into how to do all these things, we need to have a brief talk about *when* to do these things, and when not to. My own personal feelings around energy work are very strict; there are those who might complain that they are too strict, but I've seen too many things go wrong to condone a *laissez-faire* attitude toward energy work. This is dangerous stuff, kids. It's not a game, and it can mess someone up if you go into it recklessly and thoughtlessly — and sometimes even if you're experienced and go into it carefully, so tread with caution.

For me, the first part is informed consent. It's the BDSM basic for a good reason. Let's make it clear: "Consent" means that they clearly and verbally say "Yes" to the explained course of action. "Informed" means that you explained it fully and thoroughly, including the parts that could go wrong, and you are certain that they understood the explanation. Many people, upon reading this, will be taken aback by the idea that they should explain the energetic component of what they do sexually or in scene, because it's just something they do, without thinking. However, thoughtlessness is not an excuse for not examining one's behavior ... and honestly, it's usually a matter of taking advantage of the other person's lack of understanding of what is happening to them. Not everyone can feel energy work; not everyone who *can* feel it pays attention in the height of sexual or SM throes; not everyone who notices it actually recognizes it for what it is; and not everyone who recognizes it knows that it can be problematic.

You wouldn't touch a stranger with your hands without permission — we hope! — and similarly, it's not OK to touch them energetically without permission. Part of the problem seems to be that the nature of energy work — it's invisible to nearly all people and undetectable to many of them — seems to encourage beginning energy-movers to put it in a separate category from physical touch. That category is labeled "not quite real", even when the practitioners themselves would affirm that they believe it to be very real. Somehow even if you believe that you're actually doing something real (as opposed to making it all up in your head), it doesn't penetrate that this is *actually the same as touching someone with your hands*, even if they don't know it's happening.

Of course, if you're someone who would actually be physically touching people without their consent if you could get away with it, and you are reveling in the fact that you can do it energetically without people knowing, then you're a creeper who shouldn't be doing energy work anyway, and what you put out will come back to you all the faster because you are messing with something bigger than you. And the fact that you don't believe in the Law of Return ... won't help you a bit when it happens. There, soapbox over.

I would say that informed consent is a good starting point here, as with so many other BDSM dynamics. Because favea and I have different religious backgrounds (she's a liberal Christian and I'm a mish-mash of Pagan, Buddhist, Christian, and Hermetic influences), I felt it was important to discuss what I saw happening when we played. To me, the exchange of energy was naturally and necessarily spiritual and magical, and my magical ethics dictate that I get permission before messing around with someone else's life force. Also, having been on both sides of unconscious (and therefore non-consensual) energy vampirism in the past, I did not want to engage in that with my beloved.

When I've seen inappropriate energy situations in public play spaces, it has almost always been a matter of poor energy hygiene or unconscious energy vampirism. Typically, it is an onlooker who is soaking up the energy of a scene without giving anything back (think: tourist) or who disrupts the energy with their own ambivalence or suppressed desire ("Ewwww!"). I've certainly called people on that kind of behavior, particularly when I had my dungeon monitor hat on. But is that energy work per se? I wouldn't say so. I'd call it bad manners.

–Imperans, Pagan master

You'll hear people come up with all sorts of reasons for ignoring the informed consent rule, and they are all specious as far as I'm concerned, and they all seem to come down to, "If the other person actually believed/understood what I want to do to them, they'll say No!" Well, good for them for being the sort of person who has boundaries and says No ... and bad for you for wanting to use their ignorance to get your way. As soon as you stray from informed consent, you become the person they need to have boundaries in order to defend against.

Of course, this doesn't apply to a couple who has been together for years and have verbally worked out which actions require consent and which don't. But if you're not those people: Ask, explain, ask again, explain again if necessary, and take No for an answer. Also, I'd suggest taking a "Sure, whatever," that you strongly suspect isn't thought through, properly understood, or believed, as a probable No until they get to know you and your practices better. Don't take advantage of their disbelief — that's disrespectful.

–Lady Rafaella, Christian mistress

The most obvious way in which sexual energy work is problematic is that it can be energetically bonding, even when it's done one-way. Over time, a psychic bond can develop between two people that neither of them can ignore; they may feel each other's feelings (especially the negative ones) and pick up on each others' stray thoughts. While this may sound romantic, it's actually rather confusing and intrusive for both parties. It's also a serious detriment in the face of a breakup, because it doesn't stop just because the two people are angry at each other or even emotionally separated. Some psychic links are strong enough that they have to be deliberately cut by a professional energy-worker, and until then both parties will continue to experience each others' suffering. I've certainly seen long-term relationships where such a bond was a positive addition, but it is something to be entered into with caution and perhaps years of discussion — and compatibility — first.

Moving Energy

One of the things that bothered us about much of the heterocentric sexual energy teachings was the constant "gendering" of energy flows. Men were supposed to make their energy flow in this direction; women in that direction. It wasn't even that we were completely opposed to the idea that nontrans men and women might have energy proclivities that were affected by their anatomy; it was that in practice, this didn't actually seem to work. I'm pansexual and Joshua calls himself "homoflexible"; we've both dealt with the sexual energy flows of a wide range of bodies, and honestly, the direction and nature of people's energy seemed to have a lot more to do with their personalities than with their physical anatomy. Having a penis or a vagina had far less to do with it than being a "pushy" sort of person rather than someone who is more comfortable being more receptive in the relationship.

We decided to experiment, and observe our own energy flows, and those of other dominant/submissive couples. From these observations, we figured out that there are four primary ways to move energy between the bodies of people in a power dynamic. Two are dominant, and two are submissive. We call the two dominant forms "push" and "pull", and the two submissive forms "offering" and "receiving".

Before we describe them in detail, however, we should point out that we'll be talking a lot about breath and breathing in the following exercises. Breath is the pump that moves energy around the body, and in and out of it. While it's possible to move energy without harmonious breathing, it's a lot easier — and if you're not sure that you are doing it right, breathing the right way can help a great deal. Breathing together — either inhaling and exhaling at the same time, or inhaling as the other person is exhaling — can be a strong bonding activity. Breath goes in or out (another binary), but there are as many ways of breathing as there are ways of moving energy. And speaking of that, let's come back to the original subject.

Push. Push is penetrative and aggressive. It is the force of the master's will pressing into the slave's being, moving past their boundaries, and claiming the space within. On a physical and sexual level, pushing energy can be done with tongues, fingers, hands, teeth, phalluses both flesh and otherwise, and impact objects such as whips or canes. On a nonphysical level, pushing energy happens at least slightly every time the master exerts their will on the slave, and the impact of that will motivates the slave to some action. Push can be violent and forceful, or gentle but implacable. Push says, "I am coming in, and you will open yourself and accept me." If it is used unskillfully, pushing can damage the other person's energy body by disrupting and tearing it. On a purely energetic level, pushing is done with the exhale, which is self evident if you think about it.

Pull. Pull is just as aggressive in its own way, but instead of forcing the master's energy into the slave's space, pulling takes the slave's energy away for use by the master. Pull is the force of the master's will saying, "Mine!" or "No!" or "Come here!" Physically, it is the yank on the leash or the hair, and the presence that draws the slave in like a magnet and makes them willing to exhaust themselves for the master's pleasure. It is the master demonstrating that the slave's energy belongs to them, not only because they can invade it (push), but because they can take it away if they want. Push is invasion, pull is plundering. Like pushing, it can be a violent yank or a gentle teasing away of the energy. If it is used unskillfully, it can harm the other person by draining them to the point of damage. Pulling is sometimes used in healing (by skilled energy healers) in order to remove negative energies, and it is done (obviously) with the inhale.

Receiving. Receiving is the counterpart of pushing, and it requires that the slave be open and able to take and use whatever energy is given to them by the master. While most people think of receiving as merely being passive, that's not the case at all. The slave must be active in their surrender in order to best handle receiving energy. They need to be able to discern the speed and aggressiveness of the incoming energy, and adjust themselves to the dance. They need to be able to stay open — very, very open — even when subconscious parts of themselves are attempting to close down due to fear or self-protection. (We are assuming here that the slave does actually trust their master that much, and that these reactions are due to old patterns that don't apply in this situation.) Receiving is done on the inhale, and it may help the slave to be thinking "Open!" as they breathe in; and seeing themselves as a wide-open receptacle that is overjoyed to feel the master's rush of energy into their body.

Offering. Contrary to popular belief, masters sometimes enjoy it when their slaves give them energy, especially when they've had a hard day — and especially if it's given with the proper way. Offering, like Pushing, moves energy out and into the other body — but that's where the similarity ends. Offering is being an open flow, like a river, that pours generously from the slave's hands (or any other parts that touch the master). To Offer energy is not to push it on someone, but to make one's self a cup for their drinking. The energy rolls toward them like a river, but waits at their gates for them to take it.

Doing an act of Offering gracefully is harder than Receiving, because it is neither passive nor aggressive, and for some people, that binary is all that they know. A slave who is having trouble with Offering can practice with their master in this way: Focus on being an open spring bubbling up, ideally through your hands because that's usually easiest to control. Use your exhale — like Pushing, Offering is done on the out-breath. Bring your hands to the edge of your master's aura, but no further. Let the energy well up freely, but don't try to push it in any direction. Cup your hands and hold it there, on the edge of their aura. The master should wait for at least thirty seconds while the slave continues to Offer the energy, in order to give them the experience of being in that neither-aggressive-nor-passive holding pattern. Then the master should reach out and take their hands, and using their in-breath, Pull some — not all — of the slave's Offered energy from their cupped hands, and then let go. The slave should focus on refilling and holding that cup without violating the master's space. Repeat this two or three times, then on the final time establish a flow as we explain below.

Flow. The counterpart of Pushing is Receiving, and the counterpart of Pulling is Offering. As a couple, sit facing each other with your palms together. You can hold your hands up vertically or horizontally, whichever works better for you. Practice a Pushing/Receiving flow, and then a Pulling/Offering flow. While one may (or may not) feel more natural to you than the other, take the time to become familiar and reasonably skilled with both of them, as they are both useful for different things. The master should initiate the flow in both cases, because that's the master's job. If for whatever reason the master wants the slave to initiate the flow, the master should verbally cue them: "Ready? One, two, three ... go!" or something like that. This is because part of the slave's job in this work is to be able to change direction and move their energy on cue, becoming whatever the master needs them to be energetically. This sounds a lot easier than it actually is, and it can take a lifetime of perfecting. However, most slaves will find that learning to change energetic flow with the master's will can help them, subtly and over time, to be much better able to flow with the master's will in more pragmatic, day-to-day ways as well.

Once you have mastered a flow in both directions with the hands, you can try doing it through other parts of the body. Lap-sitting, in what we refer to as a "modified Yab-Yum position". The "classic" Yab-Yum — which means Father/Mother in Sanskrit — involves the woman sitting directly on the lap of the man. This modified position is used in many modern sexual energy-work traditions, and it is both gender-flexible and kinder to the less acrobatic body. One person's legs do go over the other person's legs, but either party can be on top (and usually it's the smaller, lighter, and/or more flexible one). Some couples may alternate by each having one leg on top. If either party has trouble staying upright in this position without painful prolonged tension, consider simple and comfortable bondage with rope or wide strips of cloth, wrapped around the couple's upper torso. A more informal option would be a pair of "backjacks" to sit on, so long as the seats are narrow enough so that they won't get in the way of your closeness.

When you sit face to face like this, your chakras are lined up. For those who aren't aware of chakras, they are energy points on the inner "tree", the line from your tailbone to the top of your skull. There are some arguments about how many of them exist and where they are, and which are the most important. The traditional Indian Tantric list of chakras include:

+ Root chakra (base of spine)
+ Sacral chakra (genitals)
+ Navel chakra
+ Heart chakra
+ Throat chakra
+ Third eye chakra
+ Top of head

The "Western" line of chakras includes:

- Root chakra (technically the base of spine, but includes the genitals and anus)
- Navel chakra
- Solar plexus (very important in Western magic)
- Heart chakra
- Throat chakra
- Third eye chakra
- Top of head

Pick a chakra between the root and the throat. (The upper chakras, being furthest from the genitals, are the least "intimate" and thus not the best to learn this technique with. There's also the issue that people's third eyes aren't always in the same place, which we'll get to in a moment.) If your relationship is strongly sexual and you instinctively relate through erotic energy, the root chakra is a good place to start. If your relationship is strongly romantic and emotional, try the heart chakra. The master should begin with a Push from that chakra, breathing out and Pushing into the same chakra on the slave's energy body. The slave should focus on opening up and Receiving, but when the master's "line" of energy comes in, the slave should actively try to connect with it. Once the "line" is secure, the master switches to Pulling, bringing the slave's energy back through the line to them.

(If the slave is more experienced with energy work and the master is new to all this, the slave can be the initiator, using Offering to start, and Offering again and again until the master manages to grab onto the link. Who begins is less important than the feel of the energy.)

Sit together and pass the energy back and forth in this way. If the slave has trouble knowing when the master wants them to switch, the master can cue them verbally, or with a specific touch or movement. I sometimes communicate this to my partner by leaning slightly forward or back, giving the process a long rocking motion. Once you have become comfortable with creating a flow through this chakra, try a different one — again, between the throat and root. Kissing can help to connect through the throat chakra (and going back and forth between tongue thrusting and sucking is a great way to cue energy shifts); obviously, genital arousal can help with making the connection down there. However, we advise against actual genital sex during this exercise, at least at first. It's too easy to become distracted.

When you've learned to establish a firm connection between all five of the lower chakras, go ahead and connect them all. Pass the energy back and forth between you through all five simultaneously. Remember to pay attention to your breathing! When you've mastered this exercise, you can then go on to incorporate it into some kind of face-to-face sexual activity, if that's something that interests you.

The next exercise is also done in a modified Yab-Yum position. It has four parts, each of which should be practiced equally regardless of what's most comfortable. (If you're going to do it, stretch yourself!) First, however, you need to pay more attention to your "tree" — the line of chakras going up your spine. Sitting separately, practice moving your own energy up and down the spine, using your in-breath to pump it upwards and your out-breath to bring it down. Then breathe it up through your spine and let it fall down the front of your body; after this, reverse the flow and bring it down through your spine, and breathe it up the front of your body. Some people report feeling that one direction makes them more energetic and the other direction makes them sleepier, although which is which will vary from person to person.

Once you can do this preliminary exercise with reasonable skill, get together with your partner and sit in the modified Yab-Yum position. Start by connecting with each other in the same way as above, but this time you should both focus on your "trees" as soon as you are connected. Synchronize your breathing.

First breathe the "circle", in tandem several times. Then the master breathes the circle up their back and down their front, and as it reaches their groin, uses an energetic Push to move the energy into the slave. While the master is doing that first solo circle, the slave readies themselves to Receive. When they feel the energy moving into them, they breathe it up their back and down their front, and then gently Offer it to the master, who uses the Pull to breathe it back in. Repeat so that the energy is moving in a "figure eight" between you.

Next try to join the two circles into one. Either the master starts with a Push or the slave starts with Offering, but one partner should breathe the energy out through their root chakra and into the other partner's root chakra. If the master is Pushing, the slave should open up to Receive the flow, and then breathe it up their spine. If the slave is Offering, the master should Pull the energy in and up their spine. When whoever has the flow gets it up to their throat chakra, they can breathe it back out and into the other partner, who lets it fall down their spine with an out-breath. This is especially effective when done during kissing. Alternately, you can have your heads tipped near each other, and bring the energy up to the third eye or the crown chakra, and pass it across there. When it falls to the second person's root, it gets cycled through again. Basically, it's the same as running the energy up the front and down the back of one person (or up the back and down the front) except you're using two people. After you've tried it in one direction, switch and try it moving in the other direction.

These exercises, practiced over time, help you to become more aware of energy flows between you, and also become more comfortable with deliberately moving the energy around. They are the "wax on, wax off" of mutual energy moving. If they don't feel erotic, that's all right — just use them regularly to get used to moving energy, and then apply it during sex or other activities. If they feel erotic, that's great, but don't let it distract you.

(Note: If you're playing with chakras and you notice that one person's crown chakra seems to not be present, it may be elsewhere. A small percentage of people have their crown chakras on the back of their head, near the base of the spine. We don't know why this is. But don't worry, it still works fine for all connection purposes.)

Trading Energy

For a long time, I held unwaveringly to the commandments "Thou shalt not fuck with free will" and "Thou shalt try really hard not to hurt anyone". But the Adversary is my near constant companion (and I'm not talking about Pagan fertility gods, whom I also have a great deal of respect for, I'm talking about the essence that tests and challenges us, that despite the editorial machinations of the Council of Nicea is still very much a part of the Celestial Chorus in my experience and understanding). This is the part of Unity that, when you think you have everything figured out, asks "Are you sure? It could be difficult. And there are all these other things you could be experiencing. Don't they look nice?" I always say I like a challenge, and the Universe provides. Sometimes the presence of the Adversary fortifies me to follow through with my original Intentions. Sometimes the Adversary reminds me that there is always another choice. And freedom, choice, the infinite diversity of all existence, is something that I value highly.

Since getting together with my partner Leanan Sidhe, she has been working with me on the concepts of sadism, masochism, and consensual nonconsent — concepts with which I was quite familiar from previous incarnations, but that I didn't remember until she helped me. When I am in a relationship with someone, it is my primary Intention to provide them with joy, pleasure, happiness, comfort, and safety, in whatever form they prefer. These things are the forms she prefers, so I had to make a choice. Ultimately, I chose her. I chose her because she helped me understand. She helped me understand that if someone processes pain as pleasure, then it's not really hurting. She helped me understand that if someone makes a choice to surrender, knowing full well what comes with that and being accountable for the consequences of that decision, then it's not really messing with free will, it is not taking away their choices. It is giving them the choice to let me make their choice. Using energy work to enhance our Connection, to enhance the power she has chosen to let me have over her, is an expression of this new understanding, using the tools that have served me well for much of my life. These are the different ways that it manifests:

Visual: The form that my energy takes (in my experience and that of others) varies at times between inky black shadow tendrils, purple mist, and the more common silver cords. (More common reference point for others, that is; for me the shadow tendrils are the most common.) Sometimes I use my own shadow to add more visual substance to the experience.

Tactile: I feel the energies around me as tangibly as solid physical matter. The closest I can probably come to approximating the experience for one who has never had it is holding your hand close to a television screen — but it's a less uncomfortable and more pleasurable experience, at least for me. I can feel the energy field emanating off of my subject anywhere from a few inches to a few feet depending on their level of tension (tension causes the energy field to tighten and get smaller), the strength of their presence, and the strength of our Connection. You can train yourself to notice this by holding your hands approximately four inches apart and moving them about an inch closer and an inch further away. Feel for the resistance, the pressure when you move your hands towards each other, and the pull when you move them away. This also works by holding them a similar distance from your partner, and is a good way to strengthen your Connection while training your abilities with psychometry (at least that's what I call it).

Auditory: These energies are frequently accompanied by my musical compositions, for those who have ears to listen. "I Play the Silver Strings", using the astral cords which tether our body to our soul, and tether our essence to those we have an intimate Connection with, to make beautiful music.

Effect: The effect is such that when I am most truly myself — when I am mentally centered in the otherworld, the astral, the dark places — I can tug on the Connections that I have woven through her to bring her to me; or manipulate her position to something that better facilitates my preferred angle of entry at the moment, or cause her to move in ways that are stimulating to me. These are usually accompanied by hand gestures suggestive of puppeteering. I can also perceive through the shadow tendrils that flow inside and wrap around her as easily as I can perceive through my eyes, ears, and hands; allowing me to experience her from the inside out, and to add her Perspective to my own. I use my access to her Perspective to become more adept at satisfying her desires; reaching that point at the end of the circle where pleasure becomes so overstimulating that it becomes pain, and pain becomes so intense that it becomes orgasmic. Every time that I become more intertwined inside of her, our Connection is strengthened, until we reach a point where there is no "other", there is only the communal entity that has a desire and simultaneously satisfies it, like God, like Unity, like the Universe ... like me.

–Black Sun, kinkster and energy worker

The first issue with trading energy is understanding the concept of Intent. I capitalize this word in order to make it clear that it's important. Whenever you put your energy into the body of someone else — especially someone with whom you are intimate and who trusts you, and won't be guarded — you need to focus on the "flavor" you're imparting to that energy. Most people who pass energy during sex simply flavor it with sex; if they are a romantic couple and it's done during an intimate moment, it's simply flavored with whatever sort of caring feelings they are having at the time. However, Intent can be deliberate, and it can be done as a way to get specific sorts of emotion, or even specific qualities of personality (if only temporarily) into a person's psychic system. We'll talk more about that later; for now, here is an exercise to practice trading energy.

Sit facing each other. Each of you should rub your hands together, feeling the heat and the friction. Focus on your out-breath, and focus on breathing energy out through your palms. Visualize yourself making a small ball of energy which slowly pushes your palms apart, until you are holding it between your hands. You can make it any size, but aim for something between that of a large marble and a tennis ball. Now put your Intent into it. Breathe some quality into it, visualizing it suffusing with that quality. It could be a color, like orange or sky-blue. It could be motion, like "spinning", or a smell like "citrus". It could be a more subjective quality like "courage" or "calmness". Once it has been imbued with your quality of choice, pass it to your partner's empty hand and take their energy ball in your empty hand. Try to guess the nature of their ball and have them try to guess what intent you put into yours. End the exercise by each person "breathing in" the partner's ball of energy, incorporating it into their own energy body, and seeing if absorbing it helps their ability to translate its nature.

Understand that everyone's psychic senses perceive things a little differently, and they may translate that essence very differently. Generally the brain tries to line the psychic sense up with a physical one, and thus translate the specific quality of energy into something like what the physical body has experienced, such as "buzzing" or "green" or "soft". However, our brains are different, and your partner's brain may route the sensations differently. Some people tend to get it routed to visual areas, while others might "smell" or "taste" the energy or feel it like a sensation. The meat-brain does its best to line up psychic input with physical senses, but it's not always easy. Don't be disappointed if your partner doesn't pick up exactly what you did to the energy ball, or if you don't pick up the "right" sensation from theirs. Instead, treat it like the experiment that it is. Repeat it periodically and see if the two of you get better at it. Finding out which senses their brains tend to reroute psychic feedback toward can help the process.

For more emotional qualities like the aforementioned "courage" or "calmness", however, it really doesn't matter in the end how your partner perceives it. If you imbue a ball with calmness and your partner takes it into their body, they are going to get some calmness anyway, even if they perceive the ball as "blue" and no more than that. We assume that this is because emotional states are more universal than sensory experiences, although there is no objective information on the subject. The end goal of this exercise is to learn to put emotional states into chunks of energy, which can then be passed on to the partner. Colors, smells, and tastes are simply fun ways to practice.

The third or fourth time that you try this exercise, do it a little differently. Instead of letting your partner breathe it into themselves, try inserting it yourself. For dominants, this means using "push". Push the energy ball into your submissive partner. We tend to prefer either the heart chakra or the base of the skull. Ask yourself whether this is something that you want them to "take to heart", in order to alter the emotions (in which case use the heart chakra), or whether this is a means to change their thinking (in which case use the base of the brain). For submissives, use "offering" and let your gift of energy flow gently into your dominant, and have them use "pull" to take it all the way in and integrate it. Afterwards, discuss how this felt to both of you, and what effects it had on you for the next hour or so. If one of you feels uncomfortable from the energy exchange, understand that such things will generally clear themselves out in a couple of days.

Once you become accustomed to taking in each other's energy, the two of you should agree on an Intent — a flavor of energy that you could both use — and do the back-and-forth exercise in the last chapter, only this time you should both focus on creating and strengthening that Intent. Let it pass back and forth between the two of you, becoming more intense with each turn. See how long you can keep it going. When you feel it begin to dissipate, breathe together and let it settle into you while you are both strongly connected. Wait a few hours and then report to each other on how it has affected you. How long did the feeling last? Did it shake any other emotions loose, inside you? How did it affect your feeling of connectedness? You may find it useful to keep a mutual journal of these experiments, for future reference.

Assessing Energy

This is a hard skill to learn from a book; really, it should be learned in person with a teacher and a lot of practice. In the absence of a teacher, practice will have to do. Ideally it should be practiced on a large number of people, and the practitioners should take notes and compare what they find. Unusual energy bodies should be especially noted, as you might run into those again.

First, sit and concentrate on your out-breath. Whenever we want to move parts of our energy body further out, we do it with the out-breath. When we want to bring parts of the energy body closer in, we do it with the in-breath. It seems kind of obvious, and eventually it will be second nature for you.

Look at your hands and visualize them as being gloves made of flesh, within which your energetic hands live. Take hold of a finger on one hand with your other hand, and stroke down the finger and off the end, over and over. Breathe out on each stroke. As you do this, visualize that you are slowly pulling your energetic fingers out of the ends of the flesh "gloves", and stretching them out an inch or so beyond your flesh fingertips.

Then try touching something – or someone – with the protruding ends of your energy fingers, without touching it with your flesh fingertips. If you are having trouble feeling anything as you stretch your energy fingers, you may feel a sensation when you "touch" the item or person. (Don't touch your own body – it's made of you and may not register. Another person's energy is different from your own and is more likely to register, as is an object that is frequently handled by others.) Your brain will do its best to translate these nonphysical sensations into something the physical nervous system can understand.

If you still don't feel anything, don't despair. Ask yourself "If I could feel something like this, what might this feel like?" and imagine that you are feeling it. No, you aren't actually feeling it, but sometimes with these energy exercises, repeatedly doing the action and imagining the sensation can, over many repetitions, create a mental "groove" that slowly deepens into actual reality. So keep practicing, and it's possible that (perhaps months later) your "pretend" sensation will suddenly change and become something else, something you hadn't felt before. This can indicate that a door has opened and you're actually moving your energy body around.

Once you're fairly sure that you can feel different things with those energetic fingers, lay your partner down on their back and gently "feel" their chakras with your energetic fingers. Ask them if they can feel the sensation, and how it translates to their brain. Try some of the lower chakras — the perineum, the navel, the diaphragm, the heart, the throat. Leave the higher ones alone for the moment. Note whether they are soft, hard, spongy, prickly, flaccid or strongly energetic.

If you're doing this with someone who is sexual with you, arouse them — or have them arouse themselves — and check the chakras again. Note how they change and write that down. If possible, they should then bring themselves (or be brought) to orgasm, and you should check their chakras again for comparison.

At a later date, set a time for them to focus on a thought that is distressing to them, if they are willing to allow themselves to become emotionally distressed in your presence. Check their chakras and see how they feel. This is particularly important because it's a good way to see the difference between "turned on" and "distressed". Sometimes kinky sex play runs close to the edge of those two states, and this is a good way to figure out which side of the line the person is on.

When you're done using your energetic fingertips, just inhale and "suck" them back into your physical fingertips. (I sometimes visualize a tape measure rolling up into my fingers.) If you have trouble retracting them, try shaking your hands hard and enthusiastically. If nothing else, parts of your energy body that get "stuck" in a certain shape will revert with a good night's sleep.

Over time, work on seeing how far you can extend your fingers. If you can make them turn into "tentacles" that can extend a couple of feet, that not only makes a great sex toy (there's nothing like the feeling of being "felt up" on the inside of the body) but it's useful for later exercises in this book.

Energy Work and Roles

Many people associate certain activities — sexual, work-related, lifestyle, etc. — with a dominant or submissive role, sometimes to the point where they can't imagine that someone could do X activity and still consider themselves dominant or submissive. Many of the people doing those "questionably cross-role" activities would retort that any activity can be dominant if the master/mistress gave an order that it happen, and their will rules the situation; while any activity can be submissive if it is done in a spirit of service, surrender, and "It's not about me." We happen to live on that page — it's about context and attitude, not specific activities — and throughout this book we will be trying our best to suggest both dominant and submissive ways of doing every exercise.

You may not necessarily need to arrange your energy work in these ways. For some people, the fact that one person is doing a service and the other is running the show is enough, and all "trappings" of power exchange are irrelevant to them. However, many of us got into this power dynamic stuff because we enjoy doing otherwise ordinary activities in ways that push our dominant and submissive buttons. It adds to the quality and bonding of our relationships, and it makes us hot. Sure, my slaveboy and I could certainly do anything in a completely matter-of-fact way that wouldn't strike anyone as dominant or submissive, and I'd still be in charge and he'd still have to do everything I say. But it adds that extra frisson of pleasure every time we interact, even subtly, in ways that remind us why we got into this in the first place. Given how busy our lives are, every small D/s gesture is important to us.

Basic Exercise: Grounding, Centering, and Cleansing

Before you take up practicing any serious energy work, you need to work on the basics — and by "work on them", I mean practice them regularly. The first "basic" exercise is grounding and centering. Doing this exercise on a regular basis has a number of excellent side effects. First, it runs healthy energy up and down your energetic "wiring", making you more able to move energy smoothly and efficiently over time. It can bring you down out of a freaked-out mood or even a panic attack. It can help you to sleep at night and give you energy when you're exhausted during the daytime. It helps to develop a calm center, and it is the "training wheels" for a whole host of more advanced energy exercises.

However, it doesn't fix everything right away. Getting good at energy work is a slow, long-term proposition. You may have to practice at least a couple of times a week for months before seeing serious benefits, because life is like that. It's not an instant gratification sort of thing. I often compare it to a yoga practice and tell people that no one gets from ground zero barely-fit to putting their legs behind their ears in six months. Like any athlete will tell you, you have to train. By doing this, you're beginning to train your energy body like exercise trains your physical body. Since most people aren't even aware of their energy bodies, much less moving them about deliberately, you can imagine the amount of "flab" you'll need to get through.

(Note: Some people prefer to center before they are grounded. Either way works fine. If you're having trouble grounding but the grounding gets better when you center, try centering first. I'll walk you through both types, one at a time.)

The best place to begin practicing grounding is, ideally, outside in Nature with your butt on the Earth. Even if you live in a city, finding a park or other patch of green can help. If it isn't possible — if it's the middle of winter and there's three feet of snow out, or it's pouring rain — do the best you can, but if you're having trouble, try it again in a natural setting as soon as possible.

You'll be focusing a great deal on your breath during the next several exercises. There are many ways to move energy around your body, but your breathing is the easiest and most accessible tool. In the Norse shamanic tradition in which I was trained the word for life-energy is the same as the word for breath. You'll be using your breath as a pump to move energy up and down, in and out of your body. In-breaths are used to draw it closer to the core of your being; out-breaths are used to move it further away.

Grounding and Then Centering

❖ Start with sitting in a comfortable position and close your eyes. (Some people like to say a prayer or do a small cleansing rite for the space before they begin; others just sit down and go. It's up to you.) When you get good enough at the technique, you'll be able to do it under stress, perhaps in only a few breaths. But for now, get comfortable and take your time.

❖ Take a moment to feel the edges of your body, and visualize the line from the top of your head to the base of your spine as the trunk of a tree. I like to imagine it as the trunk of Yggdrasil, the World Tree. Take three deep breaths. Focus on your exhale.

❖ On the third exhale, visualize roots coming out of your Tree, at the base of your spine. With each exhale, drop them further and further down — through the floor if you're in a building, through the floors beneath you, deep into the earth that is always under you, no matter where you are. With each exhale, drop them and spread them. Dig them into the earth. Take as long as you need in order to do this. You'll know if you are fully grounded because you'll feel "glued down" to wherever you are sitting — i.e. you could theoretically get up, but it feels as if it would be a huge effort. Don't worry if this doesn't work the first few times; keep practicing. It's not uncommon to need many repetitions to get it right.

❖ Keep focusing on your exhales. Visualize tree branches growing upward from the top of your head until they touch the sky. Don't worry about where "sky" is; just imagine it and you'll know when you've got it because there will be a feeling of connection. This centers you. In fact, you may suddenly feel your spine straighten up, because you are now poised like the World Tree between deep earth and heaven. You are the Pole From Earth To Sky, like the Maypole, like the Irminsul. You are grounded and centered.

❖ Next, sit quietly and make an assessment of your own energy levels. Do you feel generally drained, and could use some fresh energy? Or do you feel jittery and tense, with too much (perhaps negative) energy that you might like to get rid of? If it's the latter, use your out-breath to let the extra energy get pumped down through your roots and trickle off into the Earth. Don't worry about polluting Her; She can take as much as you give and transmute it. That's one of the great things about the Earth; that and the fact that it is always there under us to draw on.

❖ If instead you feel depleted — or if you feel depleted after having dumped energy — focus on your inhales. Feel, with your roots, the good green energy of the Earth. No matter where you are, the Earth is always under you, and can give you sustenance. Inhale and breathe that energy up through your roots and into the trunk of your tree. Pump it up with each inhale. Let it fill you completely, all the way to the top of your head.

❖ Once you've equalized your internal energy level, sit quietly again and take note of your Tree. Think of it as hollow, pulling up sap like a tree does, or like a pipe with liquid running through it. Think of all the tensions and annoyances of the day, the week, the month being crud that has silted up on the inside of that tube. Maybe it's even partially blocking the tube in some places. It has to go. Breathe in and pump up more Earth energy, all the way to the top of your head. As you breathe it up, visualize it swirling around and washing off the crud. By the time it gets to the top of your head, it's full of bits of crud, swirling around. Hold your breath for a count of four, holding the energy all the way at the top of your head, and watch it swirl around inside you. Then, with one big out-breath, exhale it all down through your roots into the Earth. Repeat this step three times, which ought to get out as much crud as can be removed by this method in one day.

❖ Finally, use your in-breath to pull your branches down from the sky, and then your roots up from the Earth and back into your spine. You should now feel able to move about freely. You should also feel calmer, steadier, and more able to handle anything.

Centering and Then Grounding

Sit quietly and try your best to shut off the "monkey mind", the internal chatter. Become aware of where your center of consciousness is. Straighten your spine and visualize that your spine is a pivot point around which your body rotates. Then imagine it as the pivot point around which the whole world rotates. When you feel centered in this way, continue with the exercises as above, starting with rooting. Since you are already centered, you might experiment with breathing out roots down and branches up at the same time, although this is not necessary.

Doing It Together

Try this exercise separately a few times, until you both feel that you have at least a rudimentary idea of how it works. Then try it together. You might start by doing it while facing each other, perhaps sitting and holding hands. Then try it in the modified Yab-Yum position described on page 24.

See if you can breathe your roots down together, like two trees that have grown together into one. This will mean that you will have to breathe in unison. The dominant should set the pace for breathing; think of it as a dance where there is a leader and a follower. The submissive should follow the dominant's breathing as gracefully as possible. This exercise is good practice in that art of leading and following with energy work, and it also gives both parties the experience of grounding and centering with their partner's energy intruding into their energy field. It's a prerequisite for the next step, which is learning to ground each other. However, before we go into advanced steps, we need to focus on another basic step: shielding.

Shielding and Vulnerability

When we say that someone has "shielded" themselves, we mean that they have erected a movable barrier made of energy around them. While this barrier will not keep out physical blows, light, or sound, it will — if it is done skillfully — keep out people's psychic detritus that they spray into the air around them. This is especially useful when someone is unknowingly aiming that spray at you — for example, when they are being angry, confrontational, or pushy at you. While you may still have to set good boundaries with regard to physical space or refusing to be manipulated, shielding can at least get rid of the psychic pressure and battering that can go along with that. People who have trouble setting boundaries or standing up for their own needs often find it much easier to do when they are shielded.

Some people learn instinctively, and usually unconsciously, to shield themselves. It's common for people who grew up in angry houses with lots of loud, invasive emotions battering the walls to learn shielding quickly out of sheer self-defense. (That doesn't mean that everyone in that situation learns it; some children remain unshielded and just take more damage.) Dominants are more likely to be instinctive shielders, because we like to control our environments, but not all dominant types learn to shield properly. Some submissive types find it very, very difficult to shield, because something in them desperately wants to be open and vulnerable. Others learn the hard way that people will smell "prey" on them and shield quite stoutly in order to defend themselves.

It's actually a good thing to have a submissive who can shield, because the ideal of the (sensible) dominants I know is to have someone who is only submissive to you (or to others of whom you have approved), but not to any random predator who can pull off the dominant voice. Not to mention their parents, bosses, children, ex-partners, etc. It's good if they can set not only verbal but psychic boundaries against people who have not earned their trust. However, sometimes that means they have a hard time taking down those shields in the presence of their dominant, even when both parties want them to be able to be soft and vulnerable in that safe space.

The problem with moving your energy unconsciously is that you don't control it; it controls you. If you are not entirely in control of your shielding — if it just goes on and off unconsciously depending on the randomness of your emotions, or if it's just "on" all the time you're conscious at all — then you are being robbed of your ability to choose appropriate action in the right situations. It's far better to learn — or re-learn — how to shield consciously, and then you can take them down with your partner(s) and put them up when you need to be safe.

In addition, we need to make the point that there is a difference between an "outside" shielded state and what some people have called a "contracted" state. The first kind feels emotionally like the usual sort of slight guardedness that someone takes on when they are out in public, whatever constitutes "public" for them — the job, the store, the family dinner, arguing with the cable company on the phone, etc. Submissives and slaves sometimes talk about this as "not being in my submissive (or slave) headspace", because by definition being in the submissive or slave headspace is a very open, vulnerable, and unshielded state. The other kind of shielding happens when someone feels hurt and wounded, and they "contract" into themselves. If they know how to instinctively shield, they put up an entirely different sort of shield — one that tries to repel everyone, including their dominant. This is usually not something the dominant is interested in facing, or wouldn't be if they were aware of it, which most are not. However, a contracted state can frequently be determined by checking the submissive's body language; if it's drawn in on itself, they are probably also psychically contracted.

There are a variety of ways to open a contracted state. The first way is, simply, to remove whatever mental stimulus is creating it. Most people aim for this solution, whether it be expressed through discussion and resolution of a difficult situation, or some form of physical affection or reassurance. If this doesn't work, however — or if staying contracted is an ongoing problem left over from previous trauma, and all the talking in the world won't fix it in the moment — then another method is to change the physical state of the submissive, whether they like it or not.

It's a well-researched scientific fact that the position of the body affects the brain chemistry; that's why making yourself laugh at something can actually create positive anti-depressant chemicals in your brain. Many M-types have found that ordering the s-type to physically change their stance while dealing with a difficult situation — forcing them to sit up straight, hold their head up, put their shoulders back, relax their facial muscles, etc. — can create an actual change in mood. Moving them into a more submissive posture — like putting them on their knees, or on the floor with their head between the M-type's feet, or other extremely surrendered posture — can work as well.

It won't be instantaneous — and the fact that it is not instantaneous has caused many an s-type to think, "See, this doesn't work, it's silly, and I'm still upset!" for the first few minutes. However, over a period of time this change of physical state can work, sometimes as soon as they take their focus away from how much it doesn't.

Another way to open a contracted state is to have sex. Some of the best energy work I've done with a triggery s-type has been initiated in the period directly after a session of intense sex, when they are open and relaxed and in a good mood. My s-types now know that if I roll towards them during the afterglow period with a determined look in my eye, we're going to be doing some work. They've also been around long enough, and seen enough of the track record, to know that this is a good thing.

If, after several attempts, the s-type is not able to determine the difference between a shielded safe state and a contracted state, the M-type might choose to skip this step entirely and go straight to the chapter on shielding each other. While the s-type should eventually learn to shield themselves, it might help to experience being shielded in a caring manner by someone whom they trust, in order to understand what they're supposed to be attempting on a more visceral level.

When you have an s-type with shields like a tank that almost never go down — including when they are with their M-type — there's clearly a trust problem living under there. Odds are good that it has little to nothing to do with the actual dominant they're with, but was formed by old habits and patterns that inform their dealings with everyone. (Perhaps especially every authority figure in range.) Ripping down their shields may not be the best first course; it's better to focus on ways to deal with the underlying trust problem. Some people are simply so pathologically mistrusting — usually due to early damage — that it may take years to trust enough just to be obedient, much less opening up and being vulnerable.

While there are a number of s-types with the above problem, it's actually more common for dominants to have it. The BDSM demographic encourages dominants to be steady rocks who never show their feelings (except, of course, for well-placed showings of love and affection for their submissives), let alone show vulnerabilities or struggles. Many submissives long for such a perfect rock as their dominant and are scornful of dominants who inevitably reveal their troubles and insecurities at close range. In some circles, the dominant's apparent lack of visible struggles is seen as proof that they are worth trusting with the submissive's vulnerability, and a show of internal struggle is seen as proof of their lack of trustworthiness. This social pressure encourages dominants to control but never fully deal with their problems, and it also encourages them to remain in a heavily shielded and often fairly contracted state. It may require a submissive to go a long way toward earning their trust before those shields are going to come down. While it isn't always the case, one of the best ways a submissive can earn that trust is by repeated willingness to surrender, and thus make one's self visibly harmless. Surrendering can inspire a dominant to open up, but that requires a strong, self-aware submissive who is willing to make themselves vulnerable in the first place.

At any rate, if the problem is the dominant's trust issues, by definition the dominant has to handle it themselves — and decide how badly they want to learn these exercises. A submissive can offer their help, but the nature of the power dynamic is such that they can't "fix" the dominant. Instead, the dominant can use the submissive to "fix" themselves, if they desire — a subtle distinction, but an important one.

> *Because I am an extreme introvert, favea sometimes acts as a buffer for me when we're out in public. In that sense, she conserves energy for me by creating a shield around us or by physically placing herself between me and whatever I'm finding overstimulating. (I do my own shielding, too.) I perceive our energy as partially merging for a time so that I can draw strength from her until I can be in a private space to recharge my introvert batteries. Since favea is also an introvert, I make sure that she has a chance to decompress when we get home. That usually means that we will be in the same quiet space together but not directly interacting.*

> *–Imperans, Pagan master*

To begin shielding, first ground and center as we've discussed in the relevant chapter. Once you are thoroughly grounded, use your in-breath to pull up energy from the Earth, all the way to the top of your head. (This is particularly important; most people who shield instinctively use their own energy to do it, which can cause constant minor fatigue over time. Using the Earth's energy to do it is more sustainable, because there is always plenty of it right under you.) Keep breathing the energy up until you feel "full", almost too full, ready to release some of it.

Now, with a big exhale, let the energy run out the top of your head and cascade down around you, forming a barrier somewhere between your skin and the edge of your personal space. Some people will want to push the edge of the shield far out, perhaps a foot away, but this isn't a good idea — it stretches the energy thinner and uses it up faster. People usually do this because they feel extremely unsafe on a very basic level, and it would be better to convince one's self through experience that a closer shield is just as safe. After all, it's there to stop psychic emanations, not someone's physical assault.

At this point, it can be visualized as anything you like — willow tree branches, water, fire, wind, glass, steel, whatever. Feel it make a safe space around you where no one else's angry thoughts and emotions can enter. This is shielding, and it is especially important for people living in difficult places. If it doesn't feel thick enough, repeat these last two steps and add another layer — as many as you like. (Many people learn to shield instinctively if they grew up in difficult places, but they tend to use their own energy, which is exhausting. The Earth has plenty and is not going to run out, and you can replenish your shields by doing this procedure at any time.)

You can ask a partner to test your shields. To test a shield, move your hand slowly, palm out, toward the area where the shield might be. See if you feel a resistance as you get to it. Have the shielding partner breathe out another layer, and see if the resistance grows, so you'll have something to calibrate with. If you're fairly energy-aware and the resistance flows away at the slightest touch, more layers need to be added.

Advanced Exercise: Grounding Each Other

Before you can do this exercise, you need to be able to ground yourself smoothly and well, and ground in tandem as described at the end of the basic grounding section.

This is a more advanced exercise; the person taking the active role needs to have sufficient psychic discernment to be able to feel someone else's internal energy and know how it is doing, and sufficient control of their externalized energy body to directly move someone else's.

Every master or mistress has had to cope, at least a few times, with a submissive or slave who is upset and having trouble being anything *but* upset. Obedience is not always an easy job, especially when one is asked to do challenging things, and even the best D/s or M/s relationship has bumpy moments when the s-type just has a hard time believing that it's all going to be OK. Even if the relationship isn't having problems, it's not easy to face the rest of the world armed and armored, and then have to come home and switch modes to being soft and open. External troubles can create their own trauma, and more often than not, the s-type comes to their dominant as a source of comfort and stability in an unsure world.

Obviously, the first line of defense would be to tell them to breathe and ground themselves. However, sometimes they just can't get past everything in their heads and find the focus necessary to do it. When this happens, the dominant can ground their s-type with the following procedure: Have them sit in a chair or on the floor. Stand behind them and put your hands on their shoulders. Make them breathe with you — in and out, deep breaths. Tell them to take an especially large breath, hold it, and let it out. While you are doing the breathing, extend your energetic hands (using the technique we discussed in the chapter on Assessing Energy) down through their shoulders and into their Tree, all the way to their root chakra. When the two of you do the big out-breath together, gently (gently, please!) and carefully coax their roots downward, out of their Tree and into the Earth. Keep doing this on every out-breath, focusing on rooting and spreading them, until they are grounded. Then pull yourself gently out of their body and sit down to face them, letting them focus on you. If necessary, you can verbally walk them through Earth energy exchange and cleansing at this point.

If the dominant is feeling ungrounded, jittery, spacy, or exhausted, the submissive can also act to ground them. As we've pointed out beforehand, a submissive could do that in the same position that we suggested above, and as long as both parties were well aware who was in charge and who was providing service, it wouldn't really matter. However, we found that changing our positions strengthened our connection, because it reminded us of who we were to each other. This helped us to connect deeply enough to get the work done, so it was worth putting in the "trappings".

Here are two possible positions for a D/s couple to be in when the s-type grounds their dominant. In the first position, the dominant sits with their back straight, holding their space in front of them. The s-type site behind them, legs spread, and presses up against their back. In this position, both Trees are lined up. The s-type should ground themselves, and then focus on feeling their root chakra reach out and tie into their dominant's root chakra. Using out-breaths, the s-type slowly and gently coaxes the dominant's "roots" down from their Tree, and anchors them securely in the Earth next to their own.

In the second position, the s-type grounds the dominant without being grounded themselves. Again, the dominant sits with back straight, holding their space to the front. The s-type curls up around their hips, pressing their belly against the dominant's lower back and focusing on their awareness of that root chakra against their second chakra. The s-type places a hand on the dominant's middle spine, focuses on the area between their hand and their belly, the lower half of the dominant's Tree. The s-type should breathe in deeply, hold the breath, and then let it out in one long swoop. During the out-breath, they visualize *Down!* as hard as they can. Repeat that breath and "down" visualization as many times as is necessary to get the dominant's Tree roots down to the Earth where they can plug in and get what they need.

Ideally, in both exercises, the dominant should be breathing out at the same time. Again, even though it is the s-type who is doing the work, it's better if the dominant sets the breathing pace — in this case, gentle in-breath, more forceful out-breath. For the s-type to pay attention to the dominant's breathing, literally focusing on them for every breath, helps to strengthen the connection as well as getting both partners on the same page. For both positions, since the s-type is focusing one way or another on the dominant's root chakra, it can help for them to picture themselves as a strong, low foundation for the dominant to anchor themselves against.

Shielding Each Other

While it is useful for everyone to learn to shield themselves, everyone has bad days when they are unfocused and the energy just isn't flowing right, and all too often the stress that is causing those bad days is also sabotaging the ability to make strong psychic shields. This is when a partner can step in and help. It can be wonderfully satisfying to have the feel of a partner's protection surrounding you, bolstering you against the tumult of the world. However, first I need to say something about protection, and roles.

Some of us may have a fixed idea about what it is to have someone's "protection", and what relationship those people ought to be in. However, protection — of one's body, of one's energy, of one's peace of mind — can come from any direction, including either the leader or the subordinate in any relationship. Shielding each other is about giving each other the protection of your own energy and caring. It's perfectly legitimate to have that come from either direction; it just takes on a different flavor depending on which way the energy is flowing.

When a leader shields a subordinate, the energy feels like, "I am strong and dominant, and this person is under my protection. I see their vulnerability and I respond from the same place that makes a mother bear fight for her children. I am responsible for them, and I want them to be safe." For this method, the dominant should have the submissive partner kneel, and start at their head. Stroke their heads downwards on all sides, visualizing that you are encasing them in a safe shell where they cannot be hurt. Feel the edge of their aura, and with each stroke of your hands, "harden" that edge as if you were actually making a shell around it. Work down around the entire body — you can make them stand up after you've finished with their head and perhaps even stand on a chair to get their feet, or lie down and stretch their feet up to you — concentrating on creating the shield around every part of them. (Do not shield the soles of the feet, at least at first; this is where we touch the earth and not everyone does well being shielded in that area.) Imbue the shield with your intent: *I am surrounding you, I am protecting you even when I am not present, I hold you within me at all times and you can lean on me for safety.*

We should bring up one issue here around shielding, especially if the subordinate being shielded has been generally resistant to or unable to shield themselves. Some people are psychic empaths, picking up on the emotions of others and using that information to determine how they should handle that person. (Psychic empaths may be dominants or submissives or neither, but in my experience I have run across a greater number of them on the s-side, so I begin discussing it here.) They may have done it since childhood and be completely unaware of how they "sense" these things. Some of them may depend on this sense more than on their eyes and ears. The biggest problem with this practice is that in order to be constantly taking in that information, they need to be constantly open — and vulnerable to all the horrid emotions of the people around them. While some psychic empaths have learned when to shield and make themselves safe, and when to drop shields long enough to get the information they desire, others may not be able to handle this balance gracefully.

This is especially true if they had a childhood with a difficult parent, and only their constant monitoring of the parent's emotions — and changing their behavior so as not to trigger the parent — kept them safe. On a subconscious level, they may have resigned themselves to being battered by the floating negative energy of all the less intimate people of the world in order to survive the experience of being with one difficult intimate person; and being enclosed in a shield where their normal "sense" of people's emotions is cut off makes them panic. If you as the dominant party have one of these (and you might already have figured it out because s-types with this issue often have terrible boundaries with everyone and may already be unconsciously inserting you into the slot carved by the difficult parent), your efforts to make them feel safe may have the opposite effect. Some deep work may be needed to allow them to see the pattern and figure out ways to avoid the ingrained panic. Ideally, even the most sensitive of empaths should be able to assess a situation's risk regarding information vs. safety, and shield or unshield at will depending on what will be healthiest for them; and feel equally comfortable in both situations. If that's not something that your empathic s-type can do, declare it as a goal for them, and work together on how to get there. In the meantime, try shielding them during easy situations — such as being home with family and/or friends — in order to get them used to it. For some s-types, it may also help to shield them before taking them out with you to unpleasant social situations, with the caveat that you do all the interacting and just let them float in your orbit with no expectations of people-handling. This may help to reinforce the message that being protected from nastiness can actually be a good thing. at least if there's no need for information-gathering because you're taking care of it, and them.

Protection can also be passed from subordinate to leader. Just because the President is guarded by a handful of Secret Service people who are trained to take out an assassin does not mean that they are in charge and he is the subordinate. Protection from below is the bodyguard, the knight, the vassal, the devoted retainer who guards the door to ensure the master's peace of mind. This energy feels like, "You are the one I look up to, and I want to keep you safe as you venture bravely out into the world. I would lay down my life for you. I would sacrifice myself for your peace. I will proudly guard your back, and be vigilant so that you can focus on your goal." Shielding from the bottom starts at the bottom, at the master's feet, where you — the s-type — should kneel. The best imagery we've found for this is the squire who straps on the warrior's armor. Begin with the tops of your M-type's feet and run your hands over them, or over the air about an inch away. Visualize their aura firming up and solidifying, becoming armor that protects them. Work up the legs and then the torso and arms, and end standing behind them — guarding their back — and "helmet" their head last. As you work, pour your devotion, your pride in them, and your fierce repulsion of any harmful influences into that armor. They should walk out the door feeling like they are surrounded by the good wishes of their support team, and that they can conquer the world.

Energizing Objects of Power Exchange

While not all dominant/submissive or master/slave couples have physical items that represent — and often hold the hopes and dreams of — their power dynamic relationship, many people-on-top do give their people-on-the-bottom permanent or semi-permanent collars to wear. Whether they are bought at the pet store, cut from a quick hardware-store length of chain, or made specially as a beautiful piece of jewelry, collars ritually seal the bargain of power exchange. Every time the s-type notices it around their throat, and every time their opposite number sees it catch the light, they are reminded again of who and what they are, and why they chose this relationship with this person. For many couples, the collar may be the single most important object in their home. That's why it is the most obvious target for Intent.

For the dominant partner to "charge" a collar with their Intent, they should ideally begin before it is presented. An existing collar can still be charged, and a charged collar can have additional Intent added to it if a special issue comes up, but it's easiest to begin with something that hasn't already been worn for years and filled with the energy of its wearer simply by proximity and frequency. Either way, the dominant partner should hold the collar in their hands while picturing images of their Intent in their mind. I like to rhythmically stroke objects that I am charging, for several minutes at least. I also like to chant or just repeat a specific word or phrase that is linked to my Intent and full of the right imagery.

For extra power, one can also rub body fluids into it — spit or sweat is quicker and easier, but if one wants to put in the extra effort, sexual fluids can be derived from a bit of solo "sex magic" where one visualizes the intent during masturbation and especially at the moment of orgasm. I can usually "feel" when the item is full — there's a hum or buzz or tingle to it. Different Intents for a collar may range from obvious ones like commitment or love, but they might also be qualities that will help the s-type in their role, such as discipline or strength or joy in service.

On the other side, it's not uncommon for s-types to end up caring for their dominant partner's possessions. If there's an archetypal item-interaction that is the equivalent of the collar in many power-exchange subcultures, it's the act of polishing the dominant partner's boots. This works beautifully because it involves a whole lot of rubbing anyway, and every step can channel Intent through the s-type's hands. The method is the same — hold the Intent, use chant or words if you like, mentally "push" the energy through your hands as you work them over the boots. It can be done with the boots on their owner, or empty. If you want to add sexual fluids, they can go on first and then be quickly cleaned. You can also write words in polish and then rub them into the leather. For that matter, any leather item that needs conditioning can be charged in this way — and so can fabric, especially (but not only) natural-fiber fabric. If the s-type cares for the dominant's clothing in any way beyond just stuffing them into a machine — handwashing, ironing, even folding — their Intent can be put into the fabric in this way. They can surround their dominant with love, care, strength, or whatever is appropriate.

Another substance that can be charged is food, which includes drinkables. Historical and cultural assistants who energetically charge food and/or drink for those they serve are found in numerous places; two examples that inspired us were the servants of Indian gurus and of Mongolian shamans. The babas, swamis, and gurus of India have a tradition of being very careful about who prepares their food, partly because they want someone energetically aware to put positive intent into their nourishment, and partly because of a belief that the attitude, emotions, and possibly even the character of the food-preparer rubs off on the eater of the food, especially if they are psychically sensitive. In the book *Aghor Medicine: Pollution, Death, and Healing in Northern India* (University of California Press, 2008), Ron Barrett quotes a guru telling a disciple, "...When receiving food from another, a spiritually sensitive person such as yourself will absorb some of the qualities of the person who serves you..." and later points out that "...the Aghori do not recognize intrinsic categories of ritual or social hierarchy. They do express a strong preference, however, for having their meals prepared and served by people of good character and a proper frame of mind whenever possible. I have seen Hari Baba and Pryadarshi Baba eat all manner of food without hesitation, but I have also seen each complain vociferously when disciples did not prepare a meal with the proper attention and intention (bhav) that it required. Nondiscrimination was never an excuse for a lack of discipline." (Barrett, p. 123.)

Whether or not you accept this idea, it's obvious that the best place to put conscious Intent into food is in its preparation. This can be accomplished by the s-type by chanting a particular mantra or singing a specifically chosen song while chopping and mixing and frying, or just a constant mental picture that is punctuated and passed into the food with each blow of the knife or turn of the spoon or scrape of the spatula. The M-type can specify what sort of energy they need on any given day — peace, happiness, mental strength, forcefulness, etc. — and the s-type can work on giving them energy through their food. (I highly recommend the act of the final decorative garnish as a good closure to the "spell", especially if it is edible.)

According to the late Mongolian shaman Sarangerel, the spirit-workers in her tradition created "empowered water", or *arshaan*, by calling upon their helper spirits and breathing three times into a cup of water or vodka. This could be drunk daily by the shaman to give them strength, given to clients for healing, or used as "holy water" in ritual. Some springs or other water sources automatically give *arshaan*, in the sense that their water has a stronger-than-average energetic component, but most shamans eventually need to make their own, especially if they are drinking it every day. (Sarangerel, *Riding Windhorses*, Destiny Books 2000) On a personal and household level, an s-type can charge a drink with Intent simply by holding it, breathing deeply and focusing that Intent mentally, and then exhaling onto the drink (carefully) while visualizing releasing all their Intent into the fluid. Like the shamans, you might try this three times and see how it works, although there's nothing wrong with doing as many breaths of Intent as feels appropriate.

Slave Training with Energy Work

The current literature about power dynamic relationships is largely littered with training manuals written over the past fifty to sixty years, and I'm actually fairly uncomfortable with most of them. My discomfort lays in the emphasis that so many of these training methods put on breaking the slave down and making them into a blank slate, on which presumably the master can then write whatever they like. I am not certain as to whether this emphasis comes from military boot-camp experience, or a fetish for objectification, or just not knowing any better way to do it, but it always seemed a little wrong to me. Leaving aside the ethical issues of whether it's the best thing for anyone's long-term psyche, it also seems wasteful to me, like burning down a building rather than renovating it. But then I'm a tinkerer, and I enjoy changing what is there in ways that enhance the original rather than make it completely unrecognizable.

If I was a sculptor, I would rather take the time to use and bring out the beauty of the stone with patient carving than to simply grind it up, mix it into concrete, and cast it in some industrial mold. Famous sculptors say that they don't just take a piece of wood or stone and make it into what they want — they let the wood or stone show them the shape inside, and then they peel away everything that is not that shape. It's a collusion, not a one-sided forcing of form. That's how slave training should be.

In addition, I am an animist. While I am very fortunate to have two wonderful boys who find it incredibly hot to be objectified, I am very aware that in my spiritual world view, even things have souls. As opposed to the mechanistic Skinnerian world view that inspires the aforementioned training methods, where everything is a little less than alive, in my world everything is a little more alive than it may be at first glance.

Frankly, I don't think that you can be an energy worker without eventually becoming an animist, regardless of how you see the rest of the Universe. When you can sense the energy of things other than yourself, you begin to realize that all living things have that vibrant life-energy ... and then, slowly, you begin to feel that energy in stones, in river and ocean, in fire and wind, in the earth beneath your feet. Just because the scientists say that it isn't technically alive doesn't mean that it isn't alive on an energetic level. While it might be argued that some industrially-produced man-made objects do not have that energy (and that's an argument with proponents on both sides of it), you can certainly find it in objects that were lovingly crafted, which — one upon a time — was all of them.

Having an animistic worldview radically changes my ideas about how a slave could be made into an object and trained. It doesn't rule it out altogether, but it does mean that I have to play it by animist rules. Before the age of industry, all objects were unique. Two trees might be of the same species, but they were always situated in slightly different places and would grow in different patterns. If you were to cut them down and use their wood, you had to respect its uniqueness. This tree might be full of knots that must be worked around and might be more appropriate for many small items, to cup in the hands and admire. That tree might have long, straight grain and do well as a pole to support and brace a building. Each tree had a spirit, a particular essence, that would be brought out in the carving, and with which the craftsman must come into an alliance. Similarly, each submissive is vastly different from the next one, and there can be no one single course of training that will fit all of them. The act of sculpting and polishing must be custom-planned for each one, taking into account their unique talents and hindrances.

When you shape an object that is assumed to be alive and have its own preferences, there is a connection and absorption — and perhaps one could say even a respect — that is not present when someone works with what they conceive of as a completely inanimate, soulless substance. As an animist, I expect my most valuable property to have a unique spirit. My guitar does, and so do my shamanic tools. I cannot imagine that I would want or expect less from my human property. I can even make changes to that underlying essence if I do so respectfully, in ways that honor and beautify its intrinsic nature, not simply attempt to make it into my own fantasy of what it should be.

When I craft something of wood, it will bring into its new form something of its old tree spirit, and if I craft it into a spiritual object and call a new spirit into it, I will not get to pick the nature of that new spirit. Instead, one will be drawn in which can best merge with the existing essence, and I will have to find ways to honor and connect with whatever comes. I can use my intent to affect the incoming spirit to be better predisposed toward me, but I still have to work with what I've got, and the more I understood and respected the essence of the initial piece of wood, the more I'll be able to connect with the incoming spirit. This is not unlike the situation with a human slave; the better I understand who they are in the beginning, the more I will be able to shape them in a way that is congruent with their actual spiritual destiny in this lifetime.

Changing the person's basic nature is not only wrong but an exercise in futility. All you can succeed in doing is implanting behavior so alien to their natures that the dissonance will cause them to slowly suffocate. Sometimes it may be important to implant a little alien behavior or energy — one example of where this might be useful in the non-D/s world is a Reiki attunement, where the Reiki master "scoops out" a bit of your energy and replaces it with something to aid you in doing Reiki. However, this is something to be used very sparingly, and it must never be extensive enough that it blocks the slave's own personality from coming out. The kinds of changes made in mechanistic world-view slave training force the individual's spirit down into a box, where it sits until it is released. It may never be released, but it's still there, waiting, and getting more and more cramped. Eventually, if the slave is let loose, it will reassert itself.

On the other hand, however, people are a lot more flexible than they believe. Many of the qualities that we believe are "core" to our being are actually just learned cultural behaviors that were wrapped around us at an early age, and that we are not interested in unwrapping just to see if we can. With time and patience, human beings are capable of amazing and dramatic changes, like the slow erosion of a continent. Many a consenting slave has looked in the mirror a decade after signing on, and suddenly realized how radically changed they are from the person they once were. We like to believe that everything about us is how we'll be forever, and we become shocked to realize that we can let go of things we felt were so important. That's why the slave's job is to be open to change, and not to fear it. The slave must trust their master — not to never make an error with them, because they are human, and this is setting both of you up for failure — but to use their best judgment in the matter, take into account as much as possible, and be willing to step up in the case of failure and clean up any mess that they made.

So, if we assume that mechanistic training is not appropriate for the worldview of an animist who understands the currents of energy running through the world, what is? My suggestion is that we need to begin with the idea that this is a living thing with its own preferences, and those preferences need to be gently shaped rather than yanked quickly, or sawn off. I like to think of the metaphor of a bonsai tree rather than some hideous creation made by sawing limbs off and gluing them in place. This kind of long-term sculpting requires a great deal of patience, because you are moving them gently into a position partway to the goal and encouraging them to grow into that position. Then you move a little further, and keep encouraging growth. This isn't chainsaw work, but rather something done with delicate clippers. The next section will give you some tools to help, but the first tools you need are patience and mindfulness.

Trance States

It's very useful for a master to be able to put their slave into a light trance state. While deep hypnotic trances might be fun or interesting to play with, they may be beyond the scope of the average master, and anyway that kind of hypnotic practice isn't necessary. The state that is most useful on a regular basis is calm, peaceful, a little floaty, and very open to the presence of the master. This can be achieved by simple conditioning. With the master present and sitting close, have the s-type do some meditation or breathing exercises — it can help if the master walks them through it — until they are in a calm, peaceful, and somewhat distanced state. Then the master uses a trigger on them, which is usually some sort of gesture or way of touching their body. Words can be used, but that's difficult because a specific word (or something that sounds like that word, coming through a chaotic, noisy room) can come up in conversation and set them off. Besides, a touch is so much more intimate, and so much less likely to accidentally go off when neither party wants it.

For one of my boys, I grab the back of his neck. For the other one, I grab his hair or the front of his neck. To figure out which gesture should be the trigger, I tried a number of them and asked, "How does this make you feel?" If the answer was "...sexy," or "...vulnerable," I left those alone. I was looking for words like calm, or peaceful, or a little "out of it". Next, I would have them go into that calm meditative state while sitting closely behind them, with my hand on them in that position. (It's important to get the slave used to being in that floaty, open space with the master present; if they can only achieve it when you're not around to be a distraction, that's going to be a problem. Meditating together first in a quiet room can help.)

Command Voice

When people in the military refer to the concept of "command voice", they are talking about a certain vocal intonation — perhaps combined with certain body language —

which inspires or triggers people to obey. This is the accepted definition, and I'm not looking to change it for the rest of society ... but the sort of activity that I mean when I use the term is a little different. To understand it, you might think of martial arts, where a great deal of emphasis is placed on moving *chi*, or energy, with the body. It's not enough to hit skillfully; the way to "hit harder than you hit" is to gather up *chi* and slam it out with the blow, thus affecting the target on an energetic as well as a physical level. Since your personal energy field affects your physical body (and vice versa), and since it's possible to hit the energy body with *chi* to an extent far greater than you might be able to hit the physical body with your hands (especially if you're not a large, strong person), the ability to gather and move that energy may be as important, if not more so, than the ability to strike effectively in the first place. That's why martial artists yell when they hit — the cry, or *kiai*, is used as a trigger to quickly gather and release the *chi*.

When I was a child, I did a lot of half-conscious energy moving, and I figured out at some point that if I did a particular thing with my energy while I spoke — I called it "pushing from the back of my head" — it imparted a certain energetic vibration to the words that affected people on a more-than-intellectual level. I also love to sing, and by the time I'd finished my teen years I'd taken singing lessons and sung in several choirs, so I applied this skill almost entirely to performance. When I grew brave enough to perform as a soloist, I pushed energy — laden with intent, colored by the emotion of whatever song I was singing — toward the audience. If I got it right, sometimes they cried, or told me afterwards how it had affected them in spite of themselves. I didn't question the issue of consent at that point — I was young and didn't want to think hard about tricky and ambivalent situations, and anyhow I figured that the audience had come there to have an experience, and therefore their presence constituted consent.

At some point, however, I read the science fiction series Dune by Frank Herbert, where the protagonists know how to use "the Voice" to influence people. It occurred to me that this was exactly what I was doing, although I didn't feel right about using it deliberately during one-on-one situations, except in emergencies. Later I would be trained in shamanic work, and in my particular shamanic tradition, there is a strong emphasis on singing sacred songs while pushing energy with the voice. This technique is called galdr, and it taught me a lot about how to modulate that energy down almost to a whisper when necessary. That was useful because — contrary to the military definition of "command voice" — the energetic version does not need volume to work, and indeed can be done in a whisper if necessary. Even at a quiet level, however, if it's done properly it will make someone react immediately, or at least they will have to actively check the desire to do so.

This technique, like all the others, requires practice. If you are a dominant who wants to use this technique with your subordinate partner, I highly recommend your practice with grounding, at least for the first several times. This is partially because you may end up using energy you didn't expect to spare, and there's no point in wasting your own when you're walking around on top of a battery all the time — and partially because it is important to use command voice from a stable and grounded place emotionally. Learning it while grounded reinforces that feeling, and will make it more likely that its use in emergencies will push you into a more stable place. It is also less likely that you will use it while off-balance and angry, which can have unfortunate consequences.

First, ground and center. You don't need to shield, but do cleanse and get yourself solidly planted. You are a mountain, a tall oak, the immovable and steady rock that your s-type leans on. Breathe up the good clean earth energy until you are filled with it. Then open your mouth and make a sound. You can sing a note, or moan, or whatever you like, but it should be a sound that is both relaxed and powerful, and goes on for a while. As you make your sound, let the pumped-up energy run out of your mouth on its waves. Feel it leave your body and note where it goes. (It will probably either run back down into the earth or settle into the atmosphere of the room.)

Breathe the earth energy up into your body for a second time. Again, let a sound come out of you and let the energy leave with it, but this time focus on its power. Make the sound resonant and strong. Put your intent into the energy; the intent should be *impact, strength, force.* Not anger or random flailing, but skilled mindful force, like hitting a nail exactly on the head with a hammer. While you can raise your volume for this part of the exercise, remember that you should not need to yell in order to use command voice.

Practice doing this a few more times. When you feel confident about your sound, try forming it into a single word. Use a word that you might send in the direction of your s-type — for example, "Sit," or "Down". (Again, don't bark the order. Your volume should be that of a normal conversation.) When you've practiced this thoroughly — and I recommend practicing it over a few days on your own, because you will want to see how the energy flows when you are in varying states of rest and alertness — have your s-type stand in front of you, turned away with no eye contact. Make sure that they are unshielded and open to you. Again, ground and center, pull up energy until you are full, and then hit them with both the sound and the energy of your command. See how they react, and then discuss their reaction with them. Did the command feel different? How did their body react? If the answer is "...no different," that's not a tragedy. It may mean that you need to practice more, perhaps with someone who is energy-aware in the vicinity so that they can check on your progress. It might also mean that your s-type is not very consciously energy-aware, so that they don't notice it on a conscious level, but it still might be affecting them very strongly on an unconscious level.

If your experiment is a success — meaning that they definitely notice that your command seemed to "push" them in ways beyond the simple desire to obey — then try it again, this time with them facing you. Make eye contact — which is usually a powerful thing for a couple in a power dynamic anyway — and give the command again. Discuss, afterwards, how it was similar or different to facing away and having the command come out of nowhere.

Next, rather than issuing a command, try something different with your s-type. Look them in the eye and, using command voice, tell them something positive about themselves that they find it hard to believe. Keep it simple and sincere, and personal to yourself. For example, "I find you beautiful," or "You are a great help to me," is fine, but "You aren't nearly as incompetent as you think you are," is too complex a thought, and loaded with possible negatives as well. After doing this, wait a few days and then ask them about their opinions on the matter. You may find that you have changed their self-image in some small way, perhaps without them even noticing it on a conscious level.

Words of Power

This brings us to the issue of what to say with this technique. Not every command is effective when used with this method. Command voice is best used for very simple, evocative commands that do not require a great deal of thinking or problem-solving. Complex orders are best given in an ordinary tone that does not hijack the s-type's brain, as are reassurances that could be misinterpreted by someone's subconscious or require further discussion. When composing orders or mind-shaping statements to use with command voice, I am often struck by the similarity of the kind of phrases that work well to what one might call "fairy tale rules". In fairy tales and myths, if someone speaks magic words, they aren't a long rambling sentence with lots of details about how one should or should not do something. They are short, simple, difficult to misunderstand, and evocative of specific images or emotional states. They are, in addition, generally about what should be done than what should not — "Do this!" rather than "Don't do that!"

These "fairy tale rules" work very well for conditioning a slave through verbal statements. The more positive you can make them, the better. This is especially important given that you will be using the terms during a light trance state. Trance states paradoxically make one much more open to hearing messages and taking them to heart at the same time that they take the edge off much of our cognitive precision, our ability to untangle and interpret a complex concept. "You are not a loser" can come across to the subconscious, especially in a trance state, as "...blah blah blah loser". While it's not impossible to "program" in negative commands such as "Don't ever do that!" it works better to find a way to make it a positive command, or at least a simple statement. "X makes you want to walk away from it." "Start doing X, stop immediately." "See X, think Y."

Remember that the mind — and especially the subconscious — is perfectly capable of holding two opposing statements regardless of how much sense it makes. For example, saying, "There's no reason to feel that way," won't stop any feelings. Instead, the recipient may simply feel just as bad, but then feel worse on top of it *because there's no reason to feel that way and yet they do anyhow!* It's important not to try implanting something if you're really not sure how it will reverberate through the psyche. You might try meditating or praying about a particular change you'd like to make, and ask the Universe (or however you see your Higher/Deeper Power) to send you a clear message about whether it is a good idea or not.

Shapeshifting and Phantom Limbs

From early childhood, I have had the sensation of a phantom limb, except in my case it's a penis and testicles — I have frequent trouble with gender dysphoria. Both of my masters seek to alleviate it and have taken it upon themselves to assist me as much as possible.

One of the ways they do this is by manipulating and stimulating my phantom genitalia. To me, this is a form of energy work. They are able to create sensations in me that cause reactions in the physical sense, even to the point of stimulating my phantom penis to the point that I have an orgasm, without them having laying a finger on the genitalia I was born with. It's not the same sensation as being physically stimulated, yet it is also more physically real to me than having a packer or strap-on touched. This helps tremendously with my dysphoria when I am having horrible bouts with it.

– LeananSidhe

OK, now after a whole book of not talking about kinky sex, we're going to talk about kinky sex. A little, anyway.

This subject isn't necessarily directly related to power dynamics, but I wanted to include it anyway, because a power dynamic relationship is easier on either side if a partner is not feeling terrible about their genitals. Gender dysphoria, which is caused by prenatal hormonal mis-programming of the posterior hypothalamus in the brain, causing the brain to assume for genital construction it doesn't have and sending conflicting signals, which can be crazy-making. While nothing fixes the problem (even the best surgeries are imperfect and can have problems), energy work can help with temporary relief in a lot of ways.

We hear most often about this happening spontaneously with female-bodied people who try on a strap-on dildo and use it to penetrate their lover (of whatever gender) and suddenly find that they are experiencing something more than merely sticking a piece of rubber or plastic into someone else. Their energy body, guided by their imagination and aided by the real-time-sex context, "shapeshifts" its groin area into something penis-shaped that fills the artificial cock, effectively inhabiting it for time. The brain interprets this as best it can, often giving a certain level of phantom sexual sensation. This can range from just a trace of feeling to, in rare cases, full-blown phantom sensation and orgasm.

Other gender-shifting energy activities we've heard about include people with male bodies energetically shapeshifting their perineal area (or, in rare cases of those who like to play with "sounds" — specially shaped urethral penetrating rods — their urethra) into something vulva-like for friction-sex purposes. Partners who are also energy-sensitive can discern when they are having sex with energetic genitalia — a definite sensation is felt when penetrated by an energetic cock or sliding up against an energetic vulva. Two people can simultaneously use energetic genitals instead of (or in addition to) their flesh ones.

When we say the word "shapeshifting", we generally think of werewolves and other ancient mythic creatures who changed their physical flesh into other forms. However, when it comes to actual shamanic activities, "shapeshifting" is entirely an energetic activity. Some shamans and spirit-workers use it while in trance and journeying to Otherworlds — if you're going to fly or run or fight in another world, it's easier and less distracting if you have some practice being a bird or reindeer or leopard and can relate the physical sensation of moving in an animal body to your own body, and energetic shapeshifting is the best way to practice that. Some also use it in real-time for communicating with nature spirits or entering a human body for healing purposes. Being able to move your energy body around like clay can be useful.

There are some limits on the practice — generally one has to keep the main mass of one's bodies both in the same space and lined up with the chakras, and one can only get a limited amount larger or smaller than the physical body. Some people use energetic shapeshifting for purposes of "glamour", to use the older meaning of the word that indicates an illusionary disguise. One can shrink and make one's self unnoticed, or grow taller and make one's self more intimidating or arresting. One can make one's self "brighter" and attract more attention, or "duller" and pass unnoticed in a crowd.

For those of you without gender dysphoria, who are thinking, "This chapter isn't relevant to me," keep in mind that sex which is primarily energetic can be used for other functions as well. First of all, one's genitals powering down or not functioning well due to age, hormone levels, accidents, illnesses, or the side effects of medications happens more frequently than we care to admit. Sometimes that can be helped medically, and sometimes one just has to live with it. In these situations, people can learn to shapeshift the energetic part of their genital area into a function ... whatever one wants, and work with it, including learning to have "energy orgasms". It's not the same as physical genital sex, but it can be a great experience and a fine release anyway. Practicing it now means that you'll already have it in your back pocket if something goes physically wrong.

Some prefer to practice alone at first, learning to use "phantom genitalia" through masturbation and/or fantasy. Some need the help of a partner to keep from getting distracted by their own negative thoughts, or they find the added hotness provided by a partner's physical presence (and kisses, caresses, and anything else they can give you) necessary to maintain a sexual focus.

One good thing about shapeshifted sex, as opposed to simply using your physical equipment, is that you don't need to contain everything in a realistic size or shape. Energetic phalluses can be the size of baseball bats if that's what you want.

The ends of fingers can be energetically pulled out and "shaped" into claws — and running them along the skin often creates some interesting sensations. For the lover who's always dreamed of tentacle sex, it's possible to learn to "extrude" tentacles and penetrate them. (The hands are the easiest place to do this, as an extension of the fingers, but one can extrude them from any part of the body if you've got the focus and intent.) One's entire energy body can be a toy that is always with you.

It's possible to learn how to have an energy orgasm, without the aid of genitalia. Assuming you've actually had physical orgasms in your lifetime, try moving your body in ways that it moves when it's sexually aroused and close to coming. Breathe in the way that you would breathe when you're close to coming — breath is the way we pump energy around our bodies, and breathing can be an effective "key" to trigger different kinds of shapeshifting. Make the noises that you'd make if you were physically close, assuming you do make those noises. Focus on breathing the energy down into your groin area, and with every out-breath, bear down and surge it outward just a little further. Then contract the muscles down there and send it back up with them, just a little way, with your in-breath. Combining movement, breath, muscular contraction, and energy focus (and adding in the context of a live partner who is responding to your energy) can create a pretty amazing experience.

The key is to not do it self-consciously or worry about how you're doing it. Start with no investment in it going a particular way — you're just going to play, to experiment. Don't be put off if it doesn't go well the first time, either — play with it several times before you give up. This is where imagination and being able to abandon yourself to the experience really helps — self-consciousness will close it down faster than anything else. Role-play may help some people get past their worry that this looks silly, or past a constant mental litany of "...but this isn't real!" If you actually manage to energetically shapeshift, it may not be physical, but it is definitely real. The partner who is not shapeshifting (if there is one) should concentrate on feeling their partner's energy, so that they can respond genuinely in the moment, and tell them afterwards how it felt.

There is one drawback to having frequent energetic orgasms, and that is a slow separation between the physical body and the energy body, especially in the lower chakra areas. If you've been playing with energetic sex frequently and you notice that you feel more dissociated from your genital area than usual, or that it feels numb or detached, then it's good to give it some physical orgasms (if that's physically possible for you) or at least some seriously pleasant physical sensation in order to keep everything lined up and attached. When the energy body detaches from an area, it has physical effects, including loss of muscle tone and lower immune system in that area, which can lead to infections and other problems.

So how is this useful for a power dynamic? Leaving aside the aforementioned issue that being more sexually comfortable with their body — and with their partner's interactions with that body — can increase confidence in a dominant and make a submissive feel more relaxed and willing to be vulnerable, it's possible to use the power of shapeshifting to create an energetic effect that enhances both parties' sense of the power dynamic.

First, stop thinking about your own physical body and its flaws and issues. (If you're completely fine with it and it has no flaws or issues, lucky you. Most of us aren't that lucky, and even so you might want to add a few flourishes that can't be found in normal human meat puppets.) Imagine the shape that you wish your body had, the shape that would ideally demonstrate your dominance most perfectly. Maybe it's tall and strong, maybe it's lean like a blade, maybe it's burly and impenetrable. Maybe it's not even fully human. Perhaps it has claws, fangs, horns, whatever you imagine in your head. We don't have to be realistic here. Similarly, an s-type can imagine the form that would best embody their feelings of submission and surrender. Is it childlike, or ageless? Strong, protective, and disciplined, or fragile and delicate? Whatever it is, it will be unique. Take your time imagining these forms. If your first reflexive assumption is something out of a porn novel that you've been told you ought to be like, but it actually has no affinity to who you are at your core, you might rethink it. Don't let anyone else, including media, tell you what your dominance or submission would look like if it had a physical form. Work it out yourself, in your mind. Take some days to let it blossom and define itself, if need be.

Now sit quietly with yourself. Ground and center. Starting with either your head or your hands — because that's easiest — breathe and visualize yourself shifting further toward that form with each out-breath. This should be a visceral visualization, from inside yourself — don't imagine looking at yourself from the outside; that simply distances your Intent and it won't shift your energy body. Instead, focus on how it would feel to have these arms, this face, this torso, from the inside. Lift a hand and let it move in the way it wants to move now. Get up and take a walk. You may find that you move differently when your energetic body is taking another form.

Ask this body that you've shifted into how it wants to be touched, to be handled. Think about how your partner can touch you in a way that helps to anchor you in this form, at least for a little while. Then go find your partner and describe it to them. Be that form in their presence. They may, after a time, absorb (if only on an unconscious level) that your energy body is different, and respond to it. Have some sex while in your shifted forms and see how it is different. If you've come up with ways that the partner can help anchor you in your form — a touch, a word, a position, a look — share that and try it out.

This is like putting on a uniform of dominance or submission, only it is drawn from your own deepest sense of those states, so in its own way it is more real than your physical body. Pull it out and breathe it into yourself when you need it, when you are about to enter into a situation where you'll be deeply and consciously in a state of dominance or submission.

Yes, in a 24/7 relationship it's always the background and you're always aware of it, but there are always those times when you need the extra boost.

While it's fun and can be deeply satisfying to pull out and breathe in this shape during sex, or when you're having a special evening and savoring your dynamic, the most important time to do it is when you're struggling. This goes for both sides of the slash — when the s-type is struggling with an order or part of their training or something that they want to give their M-type that is very hard for them; and also when the M-type is feeling uncertain or weak or like the weight of being in charge is about to crush them. These are the times when taking on this form can give you strength and commitment and carry you through. And really, that's more valuable to the day-to-day of a power dynamic than all the kinky sex in the world.

Advanced Workings: Healing with Energy

Energy healing is a complicated enough subject that we can only really touch on it here. I include it because people would be wondering if I didn't; but suffice it to say that my personal opinion is that it should really be taught in person, and it's not easy to learn from books. It's also deceptively easy to think that you are actually "healing" someone when you aren't, and part of learning it from a real and present skilled teacher is that they can see and check what you're doing.

I also have to give a warning about trying to use energy for physical healing in cases of serious illnesses, or emotional healing in cases of neurochemical dysregulation, in lieu of actually seeking medical help. Yes, there have been amazing recoveries from such illnesses with energy work. But they are rare, which is why they're amazing and notable, and it's quite likely that there was something else going on unbeknownst to (or at least not written about by) the practitioners. Do not stake your health and possibly your life on the hope of a near-miracle, unless you have already exhausted all other possibilities and they've sent you home to die, in which case you have nothing to lose and I wish you all the luck in the world. There, disclaimer over.

Given all this, however, it's true that many people have found that energetically intense sex has spontaneously created healing, or at least temporary relief, for chronic physical or emotional illnesses. This is more than just a good flood of endorphins that helps the person to forget there's a problem for a little while. Energetically intense sex can do a lot to bring body, mind, heart and soul closer to healthy homeostasis, but you have to trust enough to open and let it happen.

For those of us who seek power dynamics, for whom control and/or service (on either side) is quality of life, who have a deep hole in our souls when we don't have that ... arranging the energetically intense sex in a way that validates this part of ourselves gives us enough trust and safety that we can open up and let that healing in. If my s-type is going to give me healing energy — inside or outside of sex — wrapping it up in a package of service and submission is going to make me want to swallow that medicine instead of warily and instinctively shielding myself. Similarly, if I do healing on my s-types, the fact that I can surround it with my dominance and control means that they can relax and let it happen, being completely open to it. In fact, I've found that for myself, getting a small amount of healing energy from my s-type "takes" a lot better than getting a large dose from a competent, assertive professional. (Professionals, by the way, should be assertive, otherwise they can get run over by clients. It's just that I'm an alpha-type with a long history of trust-damage and I have trouble opening up to someone who isn't in a submissive position to me.)

This goes for all sorts of healings, from Reiki to psychic surgery. The most common kind of "energy healing" that we hear about often doesn't get put into that category, and that's when one partner feeds energy to their depleted opposite number, to make them feel better. This can be conscious and negotiated psychic vampirism, as Imperans recounts, or just receiving something nice to tide one over.

> *The most dramatic and obvious instances are during play and specifically when I'm fucking favea with my hand. My preferred way to use my slave is to overwhelm her senses with pain followed by repeated and/or sustained orgasm. The buildup and release of sexual energy in her orgasms allows me to pull large amounts of energy into my own body. The closest analogy I can find to describe what this feels like is the sensation of a hit of stimulants followed by a bolus of pain medication, like morphine. There is an initial "jolt" that rapidly diffuses into a warm, comforting high. Another analogy: an orgasm that begins in the brain and flows into the whole body (including, if you like, the subtle bodies/aura). If*

the energy exchange is sustained for long enough, I have profound unitive experiences, in which time becomes meaningless and my sense of self dissolves into the greater whole (the One, the All, Ain Soph, God/dess...). The sensation is by far the most intensely pleasurable I've ever felt, beyond physical orgasm or sensation-induced endorphin highs.

This process happens naturally during sex — to a greater or lesser extent, depending on the intensity of the activity — but when I am intentional about it, I can manipulate the flow of energy to maximize my pleasure, and by association, favea's. If my goal is to retain a significant amount of my slave's sexual energy in my body — either to fuel magical workings, to increase my personal energy levels, or simply for my own pleasure — I use my breath as a pump to draw the energy in, then visualize it pooling in the three cauldrons: pelvic bowl, heart center, and head. If I just want to enjoy the experience in the moment, I visualize the energy circulating up my spine and cascading down the front of my body. When I do this, I usually place my left hand on favea's heart and push some of the energy back into her at that point. (Although my left hand is usually my receptive hand, I fuck right-handed, so during sex I reverse the polarity.)

During sex, I both generate energy through intense sensation (pain/pleasure) and feed on the resulting energy. Creating and controlling sexual energy is the heart of how I dominate favea, and the core of my own satisfaction as a Master. My slave is primarily a vessel and a channel for the energy I create with her.

In a very real sense, that energy keeps me sane and functional. As a person with chronic depression, my energy levels are often low, despite a full range of treatment and self-help measures: medication, talk therapy, meditation, physical exercise, healthy diet, good sleep hygiene. Energy vampirism during sex seems to be one of the most effective ways of boosting my energy to normal or even above-normal levels. If we are not having sex often enough, I find myself less focused, less productive, and less emotionally grounded.

I do make a point of returning some of the energy to favea. Although she has never appeared to be psychically drained after I feed, I am mindful of that possibility. I sometimes get jittery after a particularly intense session, and it is easiest to send the excess energy back into her body. Typically she is so physically tired that grounding into her doesn't cause her any trouble. (It helps that she usually goes to sleep right afterward; her body has a chance to recalibrate overnight.) Alternatively, having an orgasm of my own will release enough of the excess energy to take the edge off. If even that is not enough, a shower and a snack will do the trick.

My slave and I have both observed that, in addition to keeping us cheerful, the way we use energy in sex has profoundly deepened our sense of intimacy. One of the most important expressions of submission for favea is feeling owned and used as a toy or tool for my pleasure. She derives deep satisfaction from the knowledge that being my odalisque means that I will use her sexual appetite for my own purposes — even the unusual purpose of energy vampirism — and to my own ends.

Because sexuality is such a primal part of our humanity, controlling my slave's sexual expression is a deeply spiritual act for me. It goes straight to the heart of what it means to be "one flesh" (to use the biblical phrase) as spouses. By channeling that sexual expression through energy work, we also become "one in spirit" with each other as Master and slave.

— Imperans, Pagan master

Sometimes the healing is deliberate, because one partner is trained in energy healing; or because they have been doing energy work with their partner long enough that they are able to sense when and where something is going wrong, and try things to fix it. For my own example, my own energy body tends to get ... well, rumpled up and unstrung would be a good way to put it, after heavy shamanic work, especially if there was a lot of shifting or trancework to be done.

My slaveboy is a massage therapist, and after years of us playing with energy he began to notice when I was in that shape, and began to do massages with the careful intent of redefining my energetic parts as more congruent with my physical body. "Please be feet now. Please be feet, not hooves or blobs or anything else," he'd mutter as he went. It helped a great deal, because no matter how much you play with your energetic form, it's good to spend a certain percentage of the time with your energy body congruent with your physical body, or your physical body will suffer. However, he was careful to "package" his own vibes in a very service-oriented way, in order to appeal energetically to my stubborn alpha self. Just asking my feet "please" made them relax and take in his work. It's these little trappings that help the medicine go down.

Black Sun's partner, LeananSidhe, recounts her own side of these experiences:

> *From the time I first started getting my menstrual cycle, I had severe ovarian cysts. They were bad enough that I was usually bedridden for several days. I would often sleep on the floor in the bathroom for a few days because I spent so much time vomiting that it was impractical to lie in bed, especially with it being so difficult for me to move around. I am severely allergic to the only medicine they could give me specifically for the cysts. I also refused to take extreme painkillers, due to*

my abuse of narcotics in my past. Pain, I can deal with, but not selling my soul.

Kink-wise, needles are difficult for me because of my past. They aren't a hard limit, or even a soft one for me, because if there is anything I believe in, it is staring down my fears until they run screaming away from me. Black Sun and I had been discussing the possibility of him attempting to heal my cysts for some time.

One night, we caught a scene in a movie as Black Sun was channel-surfing — I believe it was one of the Nightmare on Elm Street movies. Freddy was busy frightening some woman in black goth/punk attire. He turned the ends of his fingers into needles and rammed them into her arm, she promptly developed abscesses and died of fear, which was what he was trying to do. Black Sun and I are pretty twisted people, so the idea immediately popped into my head. I asked him if he could do that to me (the needles, not the abscesses) while we were doing energy play, because I thought it would help facilitate emotional healing for me. He suggested doing it as part of an attempt to fix my cysts.

Black Sun believes that in many ways, what we think of as destructive energy is like cancer. Not a killing force, but rather something that seeks to heal imbalances and illness and can sometimes go overboard — fixing what was wrong, but continuing to heal until the other functional parts are also wiped out. If there's anything Black Sun has in spades, it's destructive energy.

So we did it. It worked! Unbelievably, incredibly, miraculously, it worked! I believe it took two sessions to be complete (that felt like twenty), though the first one did most of the work. It hurt like hell, and it was horrifying. It was made so much easier because of Black Sun. He made me feel safe and secure, turned it into not just a painful, frightening experience — but a loving, erotic one as well. Before he removed the energetic needles, he also injected me with love. I was able to enjoy it more because I could feel his sadism getting satisfied by the experience.

I knew Black Sun could heal energetically — he'd done it for me before — but I never dreamed that I'd be rid of an affliction I'd had since I was eleven years old. Now, when I get my period, I still curse the inconvenience and dysphoria issues it causes for me. But I also thank Black Sun, thank my Gods, and thank the universe for the existence of energy healing, Black Sun's skill at using it, and being freed from my cysts. I still get cramps, but now they are usually mild to moderate. Even on the rare occasions that they are severe, they are nowhere as bad as they used to be. And I don't spend three to five days vomiting up my guts anymore — in fact there is no more nausea from my monthly cycle to speak of. It's been well over a year, so I know it's not a one-month fluke, either.

Power dynamics require deep trust, and so does healing. My slaveboy and I have taught classes to people with physical and mental disabilities about the process of using the power dynamic as an exoskeleton, a structure to hold up both parties when illness and disability is crushing them down. While such partners are rarely each others' doctors — and shouldn't be each others' therapists — there is a lot of healing to be had even in a gentle exchange of energy that is filled with the Intent of caring and trust. No matter how fortunate or how wounded you are, basking in that energy exchange can heal up the little rents and tears that everyday life inflicts on us, and sometimes, if we're willing to be open to it, it can heal something deeper as well.

Appendix: Body Congruence

(By Joshua Tenpenny, LCMT. Reprinted from Hermaphrodeities: The Transgender Spirituality Workbook. *Included for further reference about different individual energy bodies and how they can manifest.)*

The theory of Body Congruence begins with the premise that existing simultaneously with our physical body we each have a body comprised of subtle energy, roughly the same size and shape as the physical body, anchored to the physical body but distinct from it. I will call this the "astral body" for the purposes of this article, but it may also be called the subtle body, the soul, the spirit, the energy body, the body of light, or a variety of other names.

It is not necessary to be able to perceive the astral body to use most of the techniques described in this article. Your internal sense of who you are and what you "really" look like will usually match the astral body very closely. It is often the body you see when you dream about yourself. If you have no experience manipulating the astral body, most techniques can be done quite effectively by using imagination and persistence. As with most skills, while some people are naturally gifted at this, almost everyone can do it to a certain extent if they try. In some of my descriptions, I do not make a clear distinction between psychological constructs and energetic phenomenon. I do believe there is a distinction, but in practice the techniques work very similarly.

Two Bodies, Two Souls

Both traditional Chinese medicine and ancient Greek philosophy recognize a distinction between the bodily aspect of the soul which perishes with the death of the physical body, and the heavenly ("astral") or eternal aspect of the soul which can exist beyond death. If a person has an "out of body" experience of some kind, the "astral body" I am referring to is what they travel in while the physical body remains at rest. It is also the body that may travel on to the afterlife after the body dies, and if a ghost remains it is the remnants of this astral body. The "aura" is a diffuse energy field which surrounds the astral body like the atmosphere of a planet. The bodily aspect of the soul is the bio-energy which sustains the physical body. It is inseparable from it on a cellular level and animates the tissues. Without it, the flesh will rot and die.

The connection between the physical body and the astral body is much more flexible. The physical body can maintain basic metabolic processes without the astral body, and the astral body can move beyond the physical body under certain circumstances. Even so, these two bodies have a very strong natural affinity for each other. In a state of optimal health, they work together to maintain homeostasis and balance, and naturally bring themselves into line with each other. As the physical body grows and changes, the astral body naturally adapts to match it. Even though it is more malleable, changes in the astral body can also influence the physical body, generally via small neurological or biochemical alterations, affecting the metabolism, immune response, sexual response, and the chemical aspects of mood.

No one is ever in a completely optimum state of health, and substantial incongruence between the astral and physical bodies can occur. This generally occurs in one or more of the following ways: similarity, connection, stability, and definition. While transgender is primarily an issue of dissimilarity between the astral and physical bodies, other aspects of incongruence can arise due to a variety of related and unrelated factors. I will describe each one individually, but keep in mind that they often occur in combinations.

Similarity

When the physical and astral bodies are in perfect congruence, they look very much alike in shape, form, and essence. Transgendered individuals almost all have an astral body that reflects some aspect of their internal conception of their gender, although it may be more or less hermaphroditic than that internal conception. This is one of the few types of inherent dissimilarity. (Other inherent dissimilarities involve being not-quite-entirely human, and that is beyond the scope of this article.)

In general, lack of similarity is the most obtrusive type of incongruence, causing a great deal of vague discomfort that may be hard to pin down if the individual isn't aware of their astral body. Dissimilarity between the bodies can manifest as severe discomfort with the physical body and general awkwardness moving around in it, and a general lack of identification of "self" with the "flesh". There can be an urge to create alternate personas with costuming or cross-dressing, and there is often a strong desire to modify the physical body. Sexual functioning is frequently compromised, as good sex is an energetically powerful experience that requires physical body and astral body to work in harmony.

Dissimilarity may also arise over the course of a person's life when there is a sudden dramatic change to either the astral or physical body, as a result of emotionally traumatic injury, or in response to a physical change that the person is unwilling to fully accept. Adolescent growth spurts routinely cause a period of dissimilarity which resolves naturally in most young adults. For a transgendered person, the changes of puberty may be the first time they experience feelings of dissimilarity between their body and who they know themselves to be. This can cause substantial emotional turmoil which may not resolve until the person finds a way to express their inherent gender.

Dissimilarity may be caused by rapidly gaining or losing weight. A person who thinks of themselves as "fat" no matter how much weight they lose often has an astral body that is stuck at a heavier weight. The loss of a limb or other body part may cause dissimilarity, especially if the loss is sudden or traumatic or happens during a period of mental dissociation. The remaining presence of an astral limb after the physical limb is gone may contribute to the phenomenon of "phantom limb syndrome".

The most basic method of dealing with an inherent dissimilarity is acknowledging its existence. For most types of dissimilarity, this is an emotionally challenging experience, so I will give a set of exercises for that. It may be very difficult, but it can dramatically improve your ability to understand and handle the problem. This is a delicate process that may need to be done in stages. Do only as much as you are comfortable with, and come back to it in a few weeks. (Or years — however long it takes.) Don't force yourself through it.

First, become familiar with your astral body. You don't need to be able to "see" it in the occult sense (though if you can, do that instead of this visualization). Sit quietly and try to visualize the "real you". Let the image come to you, without judging that image or comparing it to your physical body. In most cases, this is what the astral body looks like, and the image has a strong feeling of rightness and realness to it. If nothing happens, spend a few minutes making a mental space for that image to be inviting it to come when it is ready, and then put the exercise aside for at least a few days.

Once you have an image of your astral body, imagine moving around in that body and going through your daily activities in that body. It should seem comfortable and real, not like a wild fantasy. Work on this until you become comfortable with that image. Can you look in the mirror and see that body? If not, imagine it. Look into the mirror inside your head, and see your real self reflected there. (Transgendered folks wrestling with issues of who they are and what they want to become may want to check out Kate Bornstein's *My Gender Workbook*.)

The next step is to become familiar with your physical body as it is. Again, try not to judge it or compare it to anything else. Just look at it, touch it, explore it. Start with area that are emotionally neutral to you, and then move on to ones that have stronger positive or negative associations. If certain areas are very difficult for you and don't want to go further, don't. Take some time to integrate the experience and come back to it at a later date. Don't attempt to like the body you see and try to feel comfortable in it. You may find that happening all on its own, but you may find you are growing even more aware of how uncomfortable you are with your body. You may even feel uncomfortable with your sense of what your astral body looks like. You may not be feeling what you think you are supposed to be feeling. Whatever your response, acknowledge it without fixating on it. Just accept that this is the body you are in at present, and it is different from your astral body. It is natural for that to be profoundly uncomfortable.

Doing both of these exercises almost always has a very strong effect on someone with substantial dissimilarity between their astral body and physical body, but it can be hard to predict what that effect will be. Some people find that when they appreciate each body for what it is, they can find forms of expression that satisfy both. If unresolved trauma contributed to the dissimilarity, this exercise may bring the person to a place of healing where the dissimilarity resolves itself. However, when the astral body has a strong inherent difference that cannot be resolved with the physical body, it is likely to cause ongoing distress unless effective coping strategies are developed.

Many transgendered people choose to resolve this dissimilarity by altering the appearance of the physical body. Temporary alterations such as hairstyles and clothing are commonly used, but some transgendered people use surgery and hormones to bring their body into closer alignment. Any of these techniques may be very successful, only partially successful, or entirely unsatisfactory, depending on the individual. The degree of dissimilarity does not reliably indicate what level of physical adaptation the person will need to feel comfortable.

For a transgendered person, dissimilarity can also occur after physical gender transition. If their astral body has adapted to their physical body as it was before transition, it may habitually hold that old form even after the body changes to a more comfortable form. This is more likely to occur with surgical changes than with hormonal changes. In hormone therapy, the body actively participates in a gradual process of physical change, and change happens only to the extent that your physiology allows. Surgical modifications are very sudden, and modify the body in a way that physiological processes cannot.

Resolving this type of dissimilarity requires reshaping the astral body to match the physical. This can be done with visualizations opposite to the ones described above. Look at your physical body, then close your eyes and picture yourself. Is it the same, or do you still see the "old you"? Imagine your physical body as it is, going about your daily activities. Stay present with whatever emotions come up. Keep working on this until you become comfortable with it. Touch your body while looking at it. Feel the shape of your body and say to yourself, "This is how my body is. This is what I look like." Don't let judgments about whether your body is good or bad come into this. You don't have to like it. Just acknowledge that it is real.

In some cases of incongruence, consciously reshaping the astral body can be useful. This is very beneficial when the difference is due to some sudden injury, or emotional trauma that has made the astral body unable to adapt. When the dissimilarity is due to something inherent to the astral body, it may be possible to reshape the astral body either to match the physical body or to a "middle ground" between them, but this is not a permanent solution. The functioning of the astral body will be impaired, and it may quickly return to its natural shape. Reshaping the astral form is an advanced technique, and best done with the assistance of someone with skill in this type of shapeshifting. If you would like to try reshaping on your own, begin by strongly imagining the intended form. Then using your hands and strong focused intent, sculpt the astral body into that shape. If the intended shape is one you have a strong affinity for, or your astral form is very malleable, this may happen fairly easily, but for most people this takes a great deal of practice and natural ability.

Connection

In a congruent set of bodies, the physical and astral are tightly connected at many points, and exchange energy freely. In a poorly connected set of bodies, there is a general feeling of disconnection to the physical world, and energy does not flow freely between them. Dissimilarity, not surprisingly, can cause disconnectedness. So can chronic physical pain or chronic emotional trauma from a young age, especially if accompanied by feelings of lack of control. The abuse of drugs and alcohol can cause disconnection, especially if used to "escape" reality. Hallucinogens and numbing drugs such as opiates are particularly dangerous in this way. In a similar fashion, disconnection can be caused by psychiatric problems of the sort that interfere with one's interface with reality — schizophrenia, severe depression, etc. And, of course, when a person is in the process of dying, the astral body disconnects from the physical.

Disconnection can manifest in a high pain threshold, to the point where the individual may not notice when they are injured. Disconnection can lead to poor digestion and a weak immune system. It often shows up in sexual problems where the person prefers to go off into their own world during sex rather than being present for it. They may think of their genitalia as an independent entity which they have little control over. People whose bodies are poorly connected tend to go easily into trance, but may find the state hard to control and they often have difficulty coming back out of it. They may appear "spacey" much of the time.

One common result of poor connection is a general disregard of the physical well-being — not bothering to eat properly or at all, ignoring the need for sleep, ignoring illness or injury until it becomes too severe to ignore. In some cases, there is thrill-seeking behavior of the sort that flippantly risks life and limb. There may even be self-injuring behavior. Sometimes these things can be used as a distraction from whatever pain has caused the disconnection, but often they seek these experiences because it they need that level of intensity for anything to feel real. Unfortunately, this is a behavior that tends to escalate, with bigger and bigger thrills needed to create the same effect. They may find a socially acceptable outlet for this in dangerous sports such as mountain climbing or skydiving, or they may prefer bar fights and reckless driving.

People who do a lot of spiritual or magical work that requires altered states and trances, journeying out of the body, or possessory work can also end up with a very loose connection between their bodies. This is particularly likely if the person's spiritual practice is very strongly focused on the spiritual to the exclusion and devaluation of the physical world. Strong connection can be maintained by spiritual practices that involve the physical body, using the physical and astral together rather than independently. Engage all the senses in your spiritual practice, using movement, touch, chanting, incense, clothing, and physical objects. Make the physical sacred.

If the disconnection is caused by physical or psychic pain, it is rarely productive to attempt to establish a connection until the source of the pain has been addressed. Sometimes this just isn't possible, and in that case disconnection and its associated problems may be preferred. It is perfectly reasonable to not want to be fully present in a body that causes you constant pain, or even constant annoying discomfort. However, if you have made considerable progress on the issue, or are in a place where you are better able to cope with it, establishing a better connection can be an important part of the healing process.

To reestablish connection in a lasting way, it is vital that you like and respect yourself. Not everyone with poor connection has this problem, but for those who do, establishing self-worth is the first step. You must want to be healthy and want to be in your body. Also, if you've been using drugs, alcohol, self-injury, sex, or any other activity to numb the pain and distract yourself from the problem, it is generally more effective to focus on those behaviors rather than working directly on astral connection.

Valuing the body and the physical world, and faithfully working at a regime to keep the body healthy and give it regular pleasure (massage, dance, walking, good food, whatever works for you) is important in retraining the mind to accept reconnection. Yoga, Tai Chi, and certain martial arts are very powerful tools for learning to use the body and energy together. Connecting deeply to earth-energy through the body, perhaps with the aid of the land-spirits, can help as well. For gender dysphoria or other issues of dissimilarity, the mapping techniques described in the dissimilarity section are also useful for strengthening connection. Connect the parts that are most congruent, and "map" the others to body landmarks and/or physical objects that can be carried on the body. Other good tools to help with connection are mindful touch, eye contact, and focused breathing with a sympathetic partner or friend.

If it has been determined to be appropriate — i.e. it won't traumatize the individual further — the astral body can be deliberately "anchored" in the physical body. This can be done through mindful touch with the intent of "locking" the two bodies together, perhaps accompanied by mindful breathing and eye contact. The five lower chakras of the body should make a very strong connection if everything is working correctly. (The upper chakras primarily connect the astral body to the outer cosmos, and do not anchor strongly to the physical body.) The acupuncture meridians can also be used for specific points of connection.

Establishing a solid connection between the astral and physical bodies may be necessary in an emergency, for instance if someone has gone into trance and is having trouble returning. Sharply pinching the upper lip can be effective in this case, as it is a connection point for the front and back energy channels. Any quick sharp pain may do the trick, the way you would slap someone who was out of control or losing consciousness. If the person has come out of a trance and is having trouble getting seated in their body, it may also help to pour cold water (ideally salt water) on the head and the back of the neck. Eating, changing clothes, or taking a shower may also help.

Stability

The physical body doesn't change quickly, though it will age over time, or become ill, or have accidents, or be altered with drugs or hormones or surgery. The subtler aspects of biochemistry and neurology may shift more quickly, but the basic physical form stays the same from minute to minute. Most people's astral bodies are also stable and keep the same form over time, with only slow and gradual changes. Some people, however, have astral bodies that shift and change rapidly, perhaps from day to day or hour to hour. Some may even be constantly moving and shifting and flickering in ways that the physical body can never replicate. This creates a continual state of incongruence between the bodies.

Constantly shifting or unstable astral bodies are rare, but usually fit into a handful of known causes. Gender-wise, the sort of transgendered individual who has a shifting astral body is often the sort with a fluid gender identity that may shift and change in response to different situations. (This can be an addition to the problems of dissimilarity and disconnection.) Someone with multiple personality disorder (now known as Dissociative Identity Disorder) will generally have an astral body that shifts when a new personality takes control. Some spirit-workers do a lot of astral shapeshifting for their work. This may lead to instability in their astral body, but it is likely their talent for shapeshifting derives from as inherently unstable astral body, rather than causing it. People with strong spiritual affinities to animal souls may continually shift their astral bodies between their animal and human forms. Many genetic psychic vampires have inherently unstable astral bodies, with many fine strands coming out through the aura.

An unstable astral body can sometimes manifest as someone who "isn't what they seem" on the outside, or who can chameleon into different personas for different situations. Some have a good deal of control over their shapeshifting; others don't, and may not even be aware of it. If stability is the only issue, and it's not causing any problems, then don't worry about fixing it. If there are problems, fortunately it's one of the easier incongruences to learn to control. Simply imagine and visualize the desired form, or energetically sculpt and mold the astral body. An unstable astral body is generally very easily shaped in this way. Holding the astral body stable in one form may be more challenging, but repeated practice and mindfulness will help. A shapeshifting astral body can be a real gift if you know how to use it properly instead of letting it run amuck on its own. The more control you can learn, the less it will trouble you.

Definition

Most people's astral bodies are well-defined, in that they seem solid, with clear edges and a definite shape. Even a very unstable form is generally well-defined, flexible yet solid. A few people, however, have astral bodies that are limp or blurry, dissolving around the edges. Like a cloud, their form has no clear edge. This is never a good thing. In most cases of a persistently poorly defined astral body, there is a poor sense of self, and there may be lifelong psychological dissociation. The individual usually has poor boundaries with others, and others' opinions and feelings; they may not be clear on where they stop and someone else begins. They may have sexual dysfunction when the person has only a vague understanding of what goes on "down there". They generally have difficulty with psychic shielding, because that requires putting a firm boundary around the edge of the aura. For that matter, they may have trouble with energy work in general, because energy flows sluggishly through them and their astral "limbs" may not be strong or well-formed enough to channel energy precisely. A person with a poorly defined astral body will tend to have weak vital energy, because without a healthy boundary, the poorly defined astral body tends to continually leak.

The vital energy can be depleted to the point where the astral body can't hold itself together, due to malnutrition, prolonged sleep deprivation, serious illness, or severe emotional strain. In these cases, the astral body is weak and thin, hanging in a thin aura that contracts closely around the body, and the chi of the physical meridians is also low. There may not be any psychological factors present in cases of severe physical exhaustion, but if this is the case, the boundary should firm back up again if the physical problem is resolved. Habitual use of narcotics or certain other drugs can also cause the astral body to blur at the edges, and this may not resolve itself if the person gets sober.

Except in these extreme cases, psychological factors are a primary cause of poor definition, and the individual may need to get professional psychological assistance to build a sense of self and deal with their boundary issues. Physical and energetic techniques can help the process, but will not create lasting change unless the psychological factors are addressed. The best thing the person can do to directly improve definition is to mindfully run their hands over their entire body on a daily basis, perhaps when bathing, with the intent of smoothing and solidifying the edges of themselves and getting a sense of who they physically are. If definition is the primary problem, this exercise might be challenging but it should also be empowering. If they can't do this exercise at least once or if it causes them distress, there is some other factor at work that should be attended to first.

Almost any type of massage or bodywork will help with developing an awareness of the physical body and its edges, which may help define the astral body edges as well. This works even better if it is done mindfully by an energy-worker massage therapist who can help solidify the astral body as they work, perhaps describing it to the client as they go along. Additionally, if the individual is inclined to learn energy work, they can start with shielding, which can help them learn to create (if only artificially) clear edges and prevent excessive energy leakage. Techniques that make them more aware of their astral body can be beneficial, but only if they are naturally inclined to that sort of work.

There are many different ways to build up low energy if this is part of the problem. Some people find a great benefit from being in nature, especially lying on the earth and connecting with that energy. Some people can supplement their vital energy by passively absorbing it in high-energy places such as music concerts, although many people with low energy will find these places overwhelming and exhausting. A few people have the skill of drawing energy directly from another person but this is not appropriate to do unless the other person volunteers. Energy treatments such as Reiki can supplement the vital energy, like a transfusion, but aren't a replacement for one's own vital energy. The Chinese practice of Qi Kung are very effective at strengthening the astral body and are easily learned by individuals who are not energetically sensitive.

Eating a whole-food diet with live foods is almost universally helpful for low energy. Eat vegetables as fresh as you can get, straight from the garden if possible. These are full of vital energy, but it dissipates fairly quickly once the vegetable is picked. Fresh unpasteurized milk is hard to obtain in many regions, but a great source of vital energy. Directly from the animal, milk has as much vital energy as blood, and unlike blood, it retains this energy for a day or more, provided it doesn't get steaming hot or freezing cold. Also very beneficial are foods that are still alive, such as sprouts, active-culture yogurt, and any fermented foods that have not been pasteurized.

In general, body congruence is an important, if much overlooked, issue of both psychic and physical health. It is valuable for practitioners of any kind of bodywork, energy work, or psychic healing to understand it in depth and be able to tell what sort of problems their clients may have with it. On the other hand, it is also important for practitioners to be humble about whether they can help the situation, or whether they should even try. If the person has complex or deeply rooted psychological concerns, it is irresponsible to assume your compassion and intuition are a substitute for training and experience in psychological counseling. Be supportive of the person's emotional experience, but ensure the person has appropriate psychological support.

Also remember that attempting to resolve problems of body congruence is not something a practitioner does to a client. It is something that they try to aid a client in doing for themselves. In all cases, the client's needs, desires, abilities, and current life situation must be taken into account. Body congruence issues don't happen without a reason, and they may not be ready to cope with that reason yet. Patience and caution is necessary; it is not something that can be forced out of season. If nothing else, the information can be given and planted like a seed that has the potential to grow in the future.

www.ingramcontent.com/pod-product-compliance
Lightning Source LLC
Chambersburg PA
CBHW022158080426
42734CB00006B/482